Leaving Candyland

by Robin Slick

1

PUBLISHER'S NOTE

This is a work of fiction. All names, characters, places, and events are the work of the author's imagination. Any resemblance to real persons, places, or events is coincidental.

Copyright © 2025 by Robin Slick
Printed in the United States of America
First edition
ISBN 13: 979-8-9915478-5-7

PECAN SPRINGS PUBLISHING

TAKING ADVENTURES, ONE PAGE AT A TIME.

https:// pecanspringspublishing.com

"We don't stop playing because we grow old. We grow old because we stop playing."
—George Bernard Shaw

Dedicated to my husband, Gary, and our kids, Eric, Natalie, Julie, and Brenna, because our family is all about love and making art.

One

Candyland is crumbling.

I walk down Penny Lane with my eyes squeezed almost shut, so I don't have to see it deteriorating in the late afternoon sun. The exterior paint is peeling, and a second-floor shutter is hanging by a thread.

And that is not even the worst of it.

You can tell the owners' priorities, though. The large front lawn and back garden are a glorious explosion of wild roses, sunflowers, begonias, sweet peas, nasturtiums, marigolds, geraniums, and carefully maintained rows of tomatoes, peppers, baby eggplants, alongside every herb imaginable.

I should know. I helped plant them.

Oh, Candyland.

It's the last split-level home in a development conceived by an eccentric Renaissance man rumored to have gone to India to study transcendental meditation with the Beatles.

We never found out if that was true, but it was enough to sell Joey and me on the place. We've lived here for over forty years. How is that even possible and why hasn't anyone figured out a way to freeze time?

When she was in elementary school, our daughter Jasmine (now known as Chef Jazz), made us a wooden sign in painstakingly drawn red and white striped letters after overhearing a classmate's mother sarcastically call our house Candyland because, as Jazz told us, we let her eat junk food and stay up late. It's still outside on the front lawn, weathered and splintered, but it still makes me smile.

Jazz originally wanted the sign to read "There Are No Rules at Candyland." Her teacher telephoned me, clucking and clutching her politically correct pearls when I laughed. I never stopped wishing I had that version of the sign instead.

Now Candyland sticks out like a toothless old woman in an intimate lingerie shop, nestled between bright rows of outrageously expensive brand-new townhomes that Joey and I joke are made of LEGOs.

As I patiently jiggle the loose door jamb, our dog Chester hears me and comes running. "Go get Daddy, Chester," I tell him through the mail slot.

Chester tries to put his tongue through the opening instead.

I stick my hand in for a kiss and he obliges. If only the world could be this way.

I'd text my husband, Joey, but unfortunately, he has a twenty-year-old flip phone with the ringer permanently off. He proudly testifies it's because he's a hippie, which is great, but honestly, I think Joey's late hippie heroes, John Lennon and Jimi Hendrix, would have embraced technology and called him a Luddite.

"Joey!" I call his name through the mail slot and bang on the door simultaneously. My efforts are met with a series of ear-piercing barks and whimpers.

Great, now Chester decides to bark.

Finally, Joey hears me and shouts, "Be right there!"

."Oh, good job, Chester, what a genius you are," I tell him.

"Hey, Linda," Joey says, opening the door. He kisses me and hugs me.

We're still sweethearts.

Joey doesn't look his age. He's built like a teenager with a full head of long, salt-and-pepper hair, and he dresses the way he did in college—jeans, sneakers, and classic rock t-shirts he buys at shows.

Joey gives me another kiss.

"How was your afternoon out? Was lunch any good?"

"Both were fine," I reply, not looking him in the eyes.

"Really?"

"Okay, I'm lying; it was awkward. I don't have anything to say to my former coworkers anymore. I've been retired for over a year, so I'm not used to being social anymore. Why, oh why, do I still get invited to these things?" I make what I hope is a grumpy face.

"They miss you," Joey remarks, ruffling my hair.

"Well, I don't miss them."

But in a way, I do. I had a cool job at the Museum of Art, where I was probably the last art major to be employed steadily with benefits for forty years. My coworkers were all art lovers like me.

And okay, I must admit these lunches are an excuse to leave the house and eat in a restaurant with someone other than Joey. Since we retired, we've been together around the clock. Not that there's anything wrong with that, although I'm finding it a little scary that the longer I stay in the house in my pajamas watching television all day, the less I feel like getting dressed and going out. I understand how older people become agoraphobic.

"What's the plan for tonight, Joey?" I ask, rubbing his back and leaning into him. "Anything good on television, or should we just listen to music? Meanwhile, something smells amazing. What are you cooking for dinner?"

"You and food," Joey says, smiling. "I'm making ravioli. No television. Bob and Marcy are coming over. Hey, that reminds me. Let's go to the kitchen because I want you to taste my sauce."

A groan escaped me—still full from lunch, and *ugh*... Bob and Marcy Garber. I should be used to it now, but honestly, I don't want to be around them tonight.

It's the same reaction I've had for decades.

We met Bob and Marcy in college and hung out mostly because our cooler friends were busy with free love or following the Grateful Dead. Joey and I always found them dull, but somehow, we ended up being each other's best people at our weddings— probably because none of us ever left Philadelphia. Bob and Marcy live in an apartment complex around twenty miles away.

When we were younger and raising our daughter, we drifted apart and maybe saw Bob and Marcy only twice a year, sometimes even at our yearly Christmas party. But once we all retired, suddenly they text and show up for dinner all the time.

I guess it's okay. It feels like all our other friends are dead, or barely living somewhere in Florida, anyway.

Our daughter lives three thousand miles away in Seattle.

I just can't believe out of all the people we've met over the years who have come and gone, we're stuck with Bob and Marcy Garber. Joey is nicer than I am. These days he gets nostalgic with them over our shared pasts whenever they come over.

I'm more in awe that we've been friends with Bob and Marcy for over forty years and still barely know who they really are.

Joey grabs a wooden spoon from a pottery jug on the counter, lifts the lid off a pan, and stirs the simmering sauce.

"Here, tell me what you think," he requests, offering me a sample.

"Oh my god," I swoon. "What's in this? It might be the best thing I've ever eaten."

Joey laughs. "You always say that."

"It's true! You are the master. And obviously, you passed your cooking genes on to our daughter."

Joey smiles like he's never heard this before. I bet I say it twice a day.

Before he retired last year, Joey was an executive chef. We have hundreds of photos of little Chef Jazz, ages three through her teens, standing next to Joey in our kitchen as his enthusiastic sous chef.

Unlike Jazz, Joey's culinary journey didn't include attending the Culinary Arts Academy or prestigious internships at places like The French Laundry and Noma. Nor did he get a phone call from the producers at *Top American Chef* and end up a finalist, enabling him to land a fabulous job and an outrageous waterfront home on Puget Sound in Seattle.

If you're someone who watches Food Television, you know we have a famous daughter. *Sigh.* A daughter on the other side of the country.

"Lots of butter, lemon juice and zest, parmesan, and garlic," Joey answers, interrupting my thoughts. I recover enough not to look at him blankly.

"You should bottle that stuff. It's freaking otherworldly," I tell him, helping myself to another taste. I'm in heaven.

But as I lift the spoon to my mouth, something wet hits me in the head and rolls down my face. I wipe it away with my hand, which is now getting soaked, too.

"Joey! What the heck is this? Do we have a leak?" I ask, pointing at the ceiling.

"Huh? What are you talking about? It must be condensation from the pasta water."

Condensation from the pasta water, Seriously? That's such a typical Joey response. Rather than admit Candyland is decomposing, he has a magical explanation instead.

I'm not having it this time.

"Condensation from pasta water, my ass! No way. Something is dripping from the ceiling! Holy hell. There's already a puddle on the floor!"

He follows my glance and is startled.

"Oh, shit!" Joey yells, turning off the stove. "Stay here! I'm going upstairs to check."

"No problem!"

I don't want to see it anyway, especially if it's coming from the bathroom.

He takes the steps two at a time. Grabbing a roll of paper towels, I try mopping up the mess, but the water keeps dripping, forming brownish pools on the floor. Joey's bargain-brand towels crumble uselessly in my hands.

Frustrated, I grab the mop, silently cursing the leak and our cheap supplies. I grab the mop instead, which I somehow step on, slamming the wooden handle into my forehead. Oh, perfect. I'm in a *Three Stooges* movie now.

I hear Joey cursing upstairs. *Please, please, please...let this not be a burst pipe or anything outrageously expensive not covered by insurance. Our finances can't take it.*

Ever since we retired and are on a fixed income, it's been one thing after another. The maintenance and repair expenses (courtesy of Candyland) are killing us. Joey returns to the kitchen with his wrench and another soggy roll of paper towels.

"Okay, all good. It's the sink. The trap is so old that it disintegrated. I temporarily shut the water off, and the drip will stop in a minute. Just don't use the sink until I can fix it tomorrow."

Ugh. In Joey World, tomorrow means three months...or never. I have depressing visions of brushing my teeth in the bathtub for the rest of my life.

Joey is awesome, but yeah, fixing things is not his forte. He's also stubborn and uncharacteristically macho about home repairs and refuses to call a handyman. Stuff breaks around here and rarely gets fixed quickly. But years have taught me to pick my fights and not sweat the small stuff.

I help myself to more of Joey's sauce and consider heading upstairs to nap before Bob and Marcy arrive. Chester, who starts barking like a maniac, thwarts my plan.

"Chester! Stop!" I yell.

"I think he hears something outside." Joey walks over to the front window, looks out, and then turns to me.

"Do we know anyone who owns a bright orange Lamborghini?"

"Huh?" I join him at the window to have a look myself, just in time to see a tall, good-looking man get out of the driver's side. He walks around the car to the passenger side and opens the door. A beautiful woman in a long white dress gets out and he takes her hand. It's like a scene from a movie.

They turn to Candyland, the man gesturing animatedly toward our house while his companion nods, her gaze unbroken.

"Okay, this is insane," I exclaim. "Should we go outside and introduce ourselves?"

"They're probably real estate investors, Linda. Let's pretend we're not home."

"They don't look like real estate people. He's got a haircut like a pop singer and she's very exotic—she reminds me of a young Cher, when she was still with Sonny. And I know real estate people are wealthy, but a Lamborghini? C'mon. Those two are celebrities. Look at how they're standing; it's like they're on a stage," I point out.

"Yes, celebrities drive up Penny Lane in a Lamborghini and stop outside our house and point," Joey laughs.

I look at him incredulously. "Joey, what do you think is happening right now? I'm…what? What are you doing?"

"They just walked up our driveway and now I can't see them, but I think they're in our yard. I'm going out there. They're trespassing on our property!" Joey grabs his jacket and goes down the short flight of steps to our back door. Chester and I follow close behind.

"Hi, can I help you?" Joey asks in what I can only describe as a strange, scary adult voice that I've never heard him use, ever.

Meanwhile, I'm transfixed. The man is handsome and obviously monied, but the woman is breathtaking. She looks like she's made of porcelain.

"Oh, hey. We didn't think anyone was home. We just wanted to get a closer look at this marvelous house. It's classic *Brady Bunch*, isn't it?"

"It's not for sale," Joey states tersely.

"I wasn't asking," the man replies, a smile tugging at his lips. His beautiful companion continues to stare at Candyland, transfixed.

"You can see the Frank Lloyd Wright influence," she remarked. "Did you know his designs are the inspiration for split levels built in the late fifties and early sixties?"

"Yeah, I'm an art buff," I admit. "Are you an architect?"

The woman laughs. "No. Far from it. I was born and raised in Philadelphia, though. And we were married at Beth Sholom Synagogue outside of Philadelphia, one of Frank Lloyd Wright's most famous buildings. Since we're in Philadelphia visiting my family and we've heard so much about your property from Ric's father, we wanted to drive over and see it. By the way, your garden is lovely. It's hard to believe this hidden oasis exists so close to downtown Philadelphia."

The man pulls a business card from his wallet and hands it to Joey. "I'm Ric Swift, and this is my wife, Natalia."

Joey looks at his card and hands it to me. I study it and almost start laughing because I was right. He's no real estate investor. His card reads "Ric Swift Studios, Nashville, TN." He's a record producer.

I called it, Top American Chef Joey. I try very hard not to smirk.

"Joey and Linda Lisser," Joey introduces, shaking his hand.

I look over at Natalia. "You're a singer, aren't you? They play your music on the college radio station I listen to. Am I right?" I must be slipping since I've retired. Of course, that's who she is. I love her music. They play it at the Whole Foods where I shop.

She blushes and nods.

I hand Ric's card back to Joey. Joey studies it again and asks Ric, "What did your father tell you about our house?"

"Oh, it was my grandfather's only foray into building. The development was wildly successful and imitated throughout the country. Does your home have a sunken living room and cathedral ceiling?" he asks

"Yep," I smile. "We love it."

"My grandfather was a visionary. After he left the building business, he was one of the first people to set up shop in Silicon Valley, California, in 1972," Ric informs.

"We heard he studied transcendental meditation with the Beatles in India," I blurt excitedly.

Don't tell me we're finally going to confirm this. Heart, be still.

Joey, meanwhile, shoots me a look that says, "These young hipsters don't care about the Beatles," which kind of breaks my heart, but I know he's right.

"The Beatles?" Ric questions. "I never heard that one, but knowing my grandfather, I suppose it could be true. How cool would that be? He was a student of T.M., I'll have to ask my dad to see if he has any more info."

Nah, nah, nah, Joey, he's a music producer, and he drives a Lamborghini. He knows who the Beatles are.

I sense they would like it if we'd invite them in for a tour. I would love to do that, and invite them in for dinner, but damn it, Bob and Marcy

17

Garber are coming over in a couple of hours. I will not expose our new cool friends to the dull-as-mud Garbers.

We stand around in awkward silence for a few seconds until Ric looks at Natalia and says, "Ready to rock, babe? Your parents are going to send out a search warrant for us," he remarks, rolling his eyes.

Natalia flashes him a warm smile before turning to Joey and me. "We'd love the chance to visit and explore the inside of your house next time we're in town. In the meantime, we'll try to discover more about Ric's grandfather. It's been such a pleasure meeting you."

"We'd invite you in now, but we have friends coming over for dinner and we need to get ready," I explain. "Maybe you can come back when our daughter is in town. You might know her. She's Chef Jazz from *Top American Chef* and Food Television."

I don't meet Joey's eyes. I know he'll make fun of me for bragging and all the proud mama stuff.

"Chef Jazz is your daughter? That's amazing—I adore her! We watched her entire season of *Top American Chef* and, naturally, rooted for her to win since she's from Philadelphia," Natalie gushes, her enthusiasm contagious. Ric flashes a warm smile at us, adding to the moment.

Yay! I'm not embarrassed to pull the celebrity card in the presence of other celebrities. If I can't use it, what good is it?

Natalia and I exchange numbers, and I promise to let her know when Jazz is in town for the holiday season. That's when she and Ric will be back in town, too.

We chat a few more minutes about music and how much we all hate the surrounding LEGO houses. Then they're back in their orange Lamborghini and driving away.

"Well, that was interesting," Joey comments, opening the back door for me.

I nodded. "Too bad we have to follow it up with an evening of Bob and Marcy Garber."

"Be nice, Linda," Joey admonishes with a smile.

"I'm always nice," I reply in my best Mae West voice. "But when I'm bad, I'm better."

Two

"That was some dinner," Bob says, patting his stomach. He's sprawled out in Chester's usual chair. I try not to laugh when I see our indignant dog giving Bob the evil eye from his unaccustomed spot on the floor.

"Thanks, dude, I aim to please," Joey quips, taking a drag off a joint and passing it to Marcy.

"How's Jasmine making out these days?" Marcy asks, exhaling. She passes the joint to me; I take a hit and hand it to Bob.

Yes, we're still children.

"Jazz is doing amazing. Seriously, we should all aspire to be her," I say with a grin. "Last week, she nonchalantly dropped this bombshell: Keith Richards and Patti Hansen asked her to cater the Stones' Seattle show. I nearly lost it. Of course, my first reaction was, 'Can Dad and I tag along as your assistants?'"

Marcy leans forward, enthralled. "What did she say?"

"Aw, of course she said 'yes', but it was that night. Even if we could get a last-minute seat on a non-stop flight, it's still six hours, three hours with the time difference, but there was no way we could do it. Trust me, I checked."

"I would have found a way to get there," Bob remarks loudly.

We all stare at him through the smoke.

Bob grimaced and shifted uncomfortably in his chair. I hoped, for a minute, that the dog's bone had somehow gotten lodged in Bob's ass. That would add excitement to an otherwise dull evening.

"What, it's the Stones," he says defensively.

"The Stones really want to be around more 65-year-olds backstage," Joey grins.

"Patti Hansen just hit sixty-five and get this—there's a photo of her on social media rocking a bikini and a grass skirt, doing the hula while flashing her Medicare card," I say, unable to keep from laughing.

"Hey, Patti Hansen just turned sixty-five. There's a picture of her on social media wearing a bikini, and a grass skirt, doing the hula and waving her Medicare card," I tell him.

Marcy fake swoons. "Patti Hansen is my idol. I'm obsessed with her Instagram account."

Bob rolls his eyes. The room becomes quiet. I feel the need to bail Marcy out.

"I know, right?" I reply. "She's so gorgeous, even without makeup or obvious plastic surgery. She looks like she has a joyous life with Keith. It's too funny that he's outlived everyone and looks better than any senior I know."

Bob leans forward in Chester's chair and leers at me like a food-crazed jackal. "You're pretty gorgeous," he practically growls.

There's another awkward silence in the room. *Oy, Bob. No.*

I guess I'm alright. I've got a good metabolism, can eat what I want without gaining weight, and I still wear my hair to my shoulders. Marcy, however, looks more like a grandmother (though she and Bob never had children). It's not that she's unattractive; it's more like she gave up and doesn't care.

I steal a glance in her direction. Her facial expression tells me nothing. She doesn't seem upset, she's just staring into space. I feel both angry on her behalf and I'm embarrassed for both of us right now.

Bob, on the other hand, is completely nonplused.

"I still can't believe you blew a chance to meet the Stones," he scolds us again.

Joey laughs to break the tension. "There'll be other times and other bands, I'm sure."

"Yeah, and we'll probably be stuck in Philadelphia for that, too," I blurt before I can stop myself.

Joey shoots me a pissed-off look. "Not this again," it says.

Yes, it's "this" again. He's right.

So here it is. In my fantasy life, we sell Candyland and move to Seattle, where we can hang out with our daughter and her very cool celebrity friends.

In reality, even if we got a great price for Candyland, all it would buy is a one-room closet in Seattle, which has a cost of living almost as high as New York City.

And let's be real. Despite her claims, Jazz has no desire to be tied down by her parents.

That's not exactly true, but it's not as if she ever stays in one place for long. Between her appearances on Food Television and at food and wine festivals across the country, Jazz has a full and crazy schedule.

But sometimes in my mind, especially if I'm a little high, I'm still the mom she begged to go with her on class trips (even in high school), the mom she called her best friend in the universe. The person she wanted to be around all the time.

Until she grew up and moved three thousand miles away.

Joey is every bit as shattered. Jazz is a "daddy's girl", too. Or was.
I get it; it's a new world out there. Kids don't live around the corner from their parents anymore. Smartphones and cheap airfare have changed the family dynamic.

It doesn't make it any easier.

"Jazz still loving her new place?" Marcy asks.

I smile; we both love living vicariously through my daughter. "Oh, hell yes, wouldn't you? Joey and I still haven't recovered from our last visit."

I flooded social media with photos of Jasmine's stunning waterfront home in Seattle—it's that cool. Honestly, I'd move there in a heartbeat, even if it meant living in the closet.

Joey, not so much. A closet wouldn't hold his collection of pots and pans, let alone his fifty-year t-shirt habit. I don't want to say my husband is a hoarder, but he's a man who cares deeply about all his possessions and has a hard time letting go. It's one of the few things we argue about, but I try not to dwell on it too much. What's the point? Accept what you cannot change, right? Right. Luckily, Marcy interrupts my train of thought before I forget that golden rule.

"Linda, we should have lunch in town tomorrow. We keep saying we're gonna do it since you retired, but I can never pin you down," Marcy whines. She's staring right into my stoned, bloodshot eyes, almost daring me to say no.

I may be high but I'm gonna stand my ground.

"Oy, I just had lunch in town today with my old office. That's my quota for the week." I reply without meeting her eyes. I look at Joey instead, who seems overly interested in patting Chester and intent on avoiding the conversation.

"How about next week, then? C'mon, you said you don't even like your former coworkers, and you had lunch with them," she pouts.

I groan inwardly. Trapped like a rat by my own lies.

"Okay, okay, next week is cool."

Please don't pin me down, please don't pin me down.

"How's Wednesday?"

I look over at Joey to save me but he's still focusing on the dog and grinning impishly. *My hero*, I think sourly.

"Wednesday is good." I force myself to get off the sofa before I make it any worse for myself, like having to pick the restaurant when I'm buzzed and not really into it.

But then I feel guilty.

"Anybody need a drink? I'm parched." I make plans to hide out in the kitchen for a few minutes. That's a sure way of keeping my mouth in neutral.

But Bob unintentionally comes to the rescue. He shifts in his chair, stretches, and yawns. "I'm bushed. Marce, are you ready to split? Long day ahead of us tomorrow."

Marcy rolls her eyes and gets to her feet.

"Yeah, a long day of nothing. I'll text you about lunch, Linda. I can't wait!"

"Same!" I force a smile and hope I don't get struck by lightning.

Three

Marcy is already seated when I arrive at the restaurant. I scan the room and grin. I told her to pick a favorite, but she chose *Terroir,* a trendy new café where everyone is at least thirty years younger than us. Perfect. We'll be invisible, free to people-watch to our hearts' content.

The moment I sit down, a server materializes, all professional timing and charm. "Hello, I'm Sean. I'll be your waiter. Can I get you ladies a cocktail?"

Sean is adorable—no, more than adorable. He's Adonis-like, with dark curls and heavy-lidded eyes. He looks about Jazz's age, though who can tell? I've completely lost perspective. All I know is that Marcy and I are acting like giddy schoolgirls. The conversation screeches to a halt as we gape at him, mouths hanging open like two fat, hungry fish. Mortifying.

"I'm Marcy, and this is Linda," Marcy croons.

I feel my face grow warm, and I wish I were home watching *Matlock* with Joey. Oy, it's going to be a long afternoon.

"I'll have a Nouveau Basilici.".

"What's that?" Marcy scans the drink menu, squinting.

Sean answers for me. "Gin, cucumber, basil, and soda water."

Marcy taps her teeth with her fingernail and stares at the drink list. "Oh. Thanks. Sorry, I forgot my reading glasses. I don't see it listed, Sean, but can I get a "Sex on the Beach"?"

Sean smiles broadly, clearly enjoying himself. "Ma'am?"

"Vodka, peach schnapps..." Marcy's voice trails off. She's caught Sean and me exchanging glances. I look down at my menu, feeling guilty.

"I'm sure our bartender can do that for you," Sean assures, with some condescension. "I'll put your drink order in and be back to tell you our specials."

Marcy swivels her head and watches as Sean speaks with diners at a table behind us. I swear I can see a bit of drool trickling from her lips. "Sean has a nice butt," she notes.

My cheeks flush as I cringe. Sean is still in earshot. I hope he didn't hear that. Even if I agree.

Marcy continues to babble. "Too bad we can't take Sean home with us, huh? Just being able to look at him across the breakfast table instead of Bob." She glances at my shocked expression.

"Okay," she remarks calmly, "we won't go there. Meanwhile, I love this place, don't you?" Marcy waves her hands around the cafe, taking in its ambiance, which is a cross between chic and a grandmother's living room. "I can't believe we haven't thought to come here sooner. We should make it a weekly thing and try somewhere new every time."

I hide behind my menu. "Oh look, they have wild parsnip fritters with fig leaf vinegar caramel and a fiddlehead salad. I won't even need Sean to tell me the specials. I'm getting that."

Marcy scratches her head, her brow furrows in confusion. "Really? You'd get that over warm shrimp salad with lemon *beurre blanc*? Or the roast chicken?"

"I can get that anytime at home. I don't even want it there. I'm a vegetarian, remember? Anyway, I need to tell Joey about vinegar caramel," I chuckle.

It's true, though I'll probably be laughing.

Marcy glances over the top of her menu, her expression resembling a dejected Basset hound. "They have a roasted beet salad with fennel pollen cream. Should I order that instead?"

I reach over and pat her hand. "I think you should get what you want," I tell her. "The shrimp and chicken dishes sound delicious."

I almost laugh at her obvious relief.

Sean arrives with our drinks. We sip them happily as he recites specials that would make me hysterical if I were watching it on television.

I order my fritters without cracking up. Marcy gets the shrimp, telling Sean, "It's not something I would have at home."

The alcohol hits us both at the same time. I'm feeling chill. Marcy looks wired, like she's going to jump out of her skin. She leans forward.

Dear lord, I hope she's not going to share something weird.

"So, how do you really like retirement, Linda? You can tell me."

Whew.

"I love it! I mean, what's not to love? Joey and I wake up every day and relax. Sometimes we watch fifty-year-old reruns of the *Match Game*; other days we take Chester to the dog park. The only bummer is that time is just flying by. When I was working, a day would last forever. Now it's just crazy how fast entire months go by. So yeah, that's the only drawback."

Marcy takes a sip of her drink and smiles. "Yeah, that, and too much time to think."

I lean back and laugh. "Think? Who thinks? That's what weed is for."

"It doesn't make you get introspective? Really? Oh well, it's moot for us. We smoke only when we go to your house."

Yeah, I know.

Marcy cocks her head and looks at me. "So, you never worry about anything?"

I frown and wave my hand impatiently. "I didn't say that, Marcy."

"Ah, sorry. It was my impression of your response."

"If it makes you feel any better, I worry about my family and money like anyone else, but I try not to go nuts over stuff out of my control."

Marcy drains the rest of her drink and looks around for Sean. "I wish I could do that. But I can't. So now I'm seeing a therapist. Because my life is shit," she whimpers.

I open my mouth and close it. Why me? Despite our lengthy friendship, it's not as if Marcy and I have ever shared anything I consider personal. I can't even recall either of us asking the other for advice. My stomach lurches; I'm not sure how to react. So, I sit there silently, feeling helpless.

"Seriously, Linda. What do we have, another ten years? Bob and I live in a tiny apartment on a fixed income. We barely exist. Surely this can't be it?"

Marcy sighs and continues. "I refuse to accept that. This can't be my life. I remember in college, my counselor told me I could be anything. And do you know what I chose?"

I know the answer to that. I wouldn't wish it on my worst enemy.

"I chose nothing," she hisses. "I fucking chose to be nothing."

Well, not exactly nothing. Marcy was a legal secretary who worked for a shyster personal injury law firm. I remember seeing her boss on television commercials at five o'clock in the morning, screaming at the camera. "Injured in an accident? Call 1-800-I AM SUING!"

My heart breaks right there. I think I hear the sound.

"Oh, my god. Not true. You aren't 'nothing'. How can you even say that?" Her words rattle me. To be our age and have such an awful opinion of yourself. To hate your life like that—I can't imagine anything worse. I try to compose myself, but tears threaten to roll at any second. My instinct is to wrap my arms around her and hug her, but it's not possible to reach across our cramped little table without setting myself on fire because of a couple of candles inexplicably lit at lunchtime.

Desperately, I twist around in my seat. *Where the hell is Sean?* Marcy and I both need another drink. *For fuck's sake, this place is tiny. Where can he be?* I look back at Marcy helplessly.

I take a deep breath and lay my hand on Marcy's arm. "I don't know what else to say, Marcy, other than I'm so sorry you feel that way. Is therapy helping?"

Marcy dabs at the corner of her eyes with her napkin. "I think so. But it's a process, and it's difficult to learn new behaviors at this age. And even harder to let go of a long-held resentment, something I thought I resolved."

"Resentment?"

She nods. "Bob."

I vaguely know Bob had a string of business failures. I feel guilty not knowing much more about it. I struggle to find the right words.

"Being in business for yourself is rough. On several occasions, investors approached Joey to open his restaurant. We were both overwhelmed with the idea and the responsibilities involved. As Joey said, we're artists, not businesspeople."

Marcy laughs. "I wasn't talking about Bob's businesses," she mutters, lowering her voice. "I was referring to his women."

Her words hit me like a slap. Women? Bob? My stomach churns at the thought. *Who would want him?* I shake my head to get the image of Bob and other women out of my mind.

I shift uneasily in my chair, wanting to know, but not wanting to know. I clear my throat. "Bob was unfaithful? Yikes! When was this?"

"It started years ago, after his appliance store went bankrupt, and he found out he was shooting blanks. I guess it was all too much for his ego to handle." She makes a face and cranes her neck, looking for Sean.

"Shooting blanks?" Through the alcohol fog, I don't understand what she's saying.

Marcy smiles sadly. "Bob found out he was sterile. We tried to have a baby for years."

Oh, jeez. I'm learning more about this woman in one hour than I knew in four decades of friendship. Maybe it's the cocktail, but she is bringing me to my knees. I could weep for her right now.

My words come out in a jumble; I can't wrap my brain around this. "Why didn't you leave him, Marcy? I mean, did you confront him? What did he say?"

"I confronted him. I got the clichéd response that it wasn't something he planned, that he 'loves me and will never do it again.' It wasn't so much that I believed him…that's not the reason I stayed; it was more that I understood why."

I lean closer. "You did? Really?"

Marcy toys with her napkin, then looks up, tears shimmering in her eyes. "Yeah. He felt like a loser. His business crashed, we declared bankruptcy and lost our house. All at the same time, he finds out he'll never be a father and it's his fault, his bum sperm."

I grit my teeth. Bob's excuses don't wash. "But what about you, Marcy? You lost your house and dream of a child, too! And then he cheats on you?" I shake my head, angry. "I'm not sure I can look at him ever again." I mean this; I do. I'm wounded on behalf of this woman. I feel like throwing up.

Marcy rests her hand gently on mine. "It's okay, Linda. It is. I understood where he was coming from—times were different then. Bob… well, he's just a poor, pathetic soul. I thought about leaving him, but I know in his clumsy way that he loves me."

She laughs harshly. "Really, who would want me, anyway?" Marcy takes a sip of her drink and continues. "Well, someone wanted me, and if Bob hadn't been unfaithful, I never would have met the great love of my life."

I sit up straight in my chair and grab the remnants of my drink. *Feh.* It's nothing but melted ice. Where is that waiter?

I subtly pull on my ears to check if they're blocked. There's no way I heard that correctly. "You had an affair?"

"I did. For almost twenty years, can you believe it? It started when I turned thirty. I thought it was going to last forever. It devastated me when it ended. But you know the expression, it's better to have loved and lost, *blah, blah, blah.* Anyway, my therapist thinks my anger and resentment toward Bob isn't his womanizing, since that would be beyond hypocritical, but more because I'm not ready to call it a life yet, and it seems like Bob already has. I feel like we just…exist; we're not living. I know what it feels to be alive, and I want to feel that way again before I die."

I prop my elbows on the table and rest my chin on my hands. The conversation is becoming interesting. "So, what are you saying exactly? What is it you want?"

Marcy laughs. "If I knew, I wouldn't need therapy."

Now it's my turn to laugh. "Good point. I have to ask. What ended up happening with your lover? Did he ask you to leave, Bob and you couldn't do it?" I'm not sure why this question pops into my head. I'm still digesting the idea of mousy little Marcy having a twenty-year affair.

"No," she mutters, with a look of pure agony.

Oh crap. He dumped her. Or maybe it was something else.

"Ah. Wasn't he available? Was he married, too?"

Marcy stares helplessly at her empty drink for what feels like forever before finally responding.

"Yes. Yes, he was married. He was unavailable, he made that clear."

I swirl the melting ice in my glass before taking a swig. *What the hell do I say now?* "Oh. I'm sorry. That sucks. This sounds like a bad romance novel. But what about now? If you're that unhappy with your life, why don't you leave Bob?"

Marcy grimaces. "Because, as nuts as it sounds, I still have feelings for him. We have a history. You, of all people, can understand that, right? I can't just walk away from a lifetime together. I'm sixty-five years old and on eight different medications for my heart and high blood pressure. I don't want to be old and sick and all alone. Don't you ever worry about that? Don't you ever look at Joey and wonder what would happen to you if he…you know…" She stares into my eyes intently, waiting for my reply. All I'm thinking is, *Marcy, please don't put these thoughts in my head.*

But I shrug and try to speak calmly. "I don't live like that, Marcy. It's unnecessary suffering. None of us has a guarantee. We could be here just another second or hang on twenty more years. I live joyously every day." I hope I sound convincing, but I'm not sure I believe what I'm saying either.

Marcy looks at me sadly. "I never thought about losing someone I thought I couldn't live without either," she reflects. "Until…until it happened."

This is completely freaking me out. I know I shouldn't ask, but I can't help myself.

"Who was it?" I blurt. "Was it anyone I would know?"

Marcy breathes in and out slowly and chews on her bottom lip. "Actually, yes. It's someone you know," she whispers.

Heat rushes to my face, and the room spins. I grip the table, trying to steady myself.

Four

The last time I felt like this was when I got the call my mother had died.

I was a sophomore in college, living in a dorm not too far from home. My father telephoned. It was before cell phones, so I had to take the call in the resident hall director's office.

My dad was talking to me, I know he was, but he sounded far away, and his words made no sense. I must have subliminally understood what he was trying to tell me, though. I heard a loud buzzing noise in my ears, and the room spun. It was beyond shocking. My father could barely keep it together, sobbing as he told me that Mom, who was in perfect health, died of a heart attack in her sleep.

The sweat poured off me. It was like I stepped outside of my body. Death happened in other families, not mine.

Incredibly, my father passed away from a fatal cardiac arrest just two months later. I firmly believe it was because of a broken heart after losing his beloved wife. I was blind with grief and considered dropping out of school. Luckily, I was already talking with a counselor at school after my mother's death. My counselor gave me what she called a crash course in "kind of" Buddhism, which enabled me to deal with losing them. To this day, I believe that consciousness, or spirit, continues after death and can be reborn.

I see my parents in Jazz all the time, though to be honest, sometimes I see them in our dog, Chester, too.

Hey, it's possible. Anything is.

Joey and I met at a grief support group recommended by said counselor, who I swear played matchmaker to the two of us.

Joey was raised by a single mom named Judy, who died right around the same time as my father. Even though Joey insisted he was fine, he went to one meeting so he could confirm to our grief counselor he was indeed okay. That's when he first saw me, sobbing by myself in the back row of seats.

It was one of those love-at-first-sight things.

No, it was.

We had everything in common — a love of art, music, and food — but really, we immediately liked each other and were extremely physically attracted. We went out for a beer after the meeting. I don't think we were ever apart again. We became Linda-Joey, joined spiritually at the hip.

Were we especially vulnerable to falling in love so young because we shared being orphaned almost simultaneously? Maybe. We both think it would have happened anyway. Destiny is a thing.

Oh, how I wish Joey had met my mother and father.

What can I say about my parents other than that I took them for granted, thinking they'd live forever? I didn't realize how much I missed them until years after they were gone, and I had a daughter of my own.

My mother and father were almost forty when I was born, which was a total anomaly back then. They had friends just a few years older who were already grandparents. But really, the whole parent/child dynamic was different in the fifties and sixties. Parents were parents, not confidants or friends. They didn't ask us for our opinions, they didn't hover over us. Our only job was to play outside all day and be home in time for dinner.

My parents weren't cool or wealthy. However, I had a closet full of clothes and was never hungry, even if our vegetables came out of a box and my mom's cooking spices of choice were either Lipton onion soup mix or a can of ginger ale.

So yeah, I thought my parents were dull and establishment. They lived in the same house for thirty years and vacationed every summer the same week at a cramped rental in Ocean City, New Jersey.

But oh, I know they loved me.

And to this day, I feel guilty about all the times during my childhood I vowed to be nothing like them when I grew up.

The joke is on me, huh?

Anyway, thinking of my parents and the past makes me sad and doesn't jibe with my blurry idea of Buddhism, so I don't do it.

Until I have lunch with Marcy, that is.

Marcy grabs my hand and gives it a little shake. "Linda! Are you okay?"

I'm fine. I blink rapidly, trying to steady my vision and my racing heart. "Yeah, it just got a little hot in here, and I'm hungry. I should never drink on an empty stomach."

"Wow, you scared me for a second. You went all pale, like you saw a ghost."

"Well, honestly, you shocked me when you said your lover is someone I know. "Marcy's smile fades into a sad curl as she twirls her napkin between her fingers.

"Well, I should have said it's someone you knew. He's no longer with us." Her eyes tear up, and she wipes them with her sleeve.

I exhale slowly. Is it the giddy relief I'm feeling, or is it simply nausea from alcohol and no food?

"Who was it, Marcy?"

Marcy hesitates, her fingers nervously twisting her napkin into knots. My heart pounds as she takes a deep breath, locking eyes with me. "Claude Bissonette."

At first, I think I heard her wrong. Because what I think I heard isn't possible.

"Who?" I ask, my voice quavering.

"Claude Bissonette."

"Dr. Bissonette? My boss? You had an affair with my boss?"

If I were a cartoon, my head would spin around and around. Wait, I think it is! I put my chin in my hand to steady it. I'm shaking.

Of course, *now* Sean finally appears with our food and covers his mouth with one hand when he sees our empty glasses. He sets down our lunch and smiles at us a little guiltily. At least this causes me to snap out of it, and I feel better. There's something sweet about him. I can't describe it.

"Another round, ladies?"

"Yes!" We shout in unison.

Marcy picks up her fork and stabs her shrimp enthusiastically.

I, however, seem to have lost my appetite.

Holy hell, Marcy had a twenty-year affair with my former boss, the president of the Museum of Art?

This reeks of tragedy. Dr. Claude Bissonette took his life around ten years ago, a couple of years after he resigned from his position and retired to Mexico. His suicide was shocking. My coworkers and I grieved and tried to make sense of it for months.

It occurs that Marcy can give me insight and answers to so many questions about what happened, but I don't have the stomach for it now.

"How are your fritters?" Marcy questions, chewing her shrimp with gusto. "Did you even try them yet?"

That's it; really? We're done talking about Dr. Bissonette now? I watch in disbelief as Marcy shoves another forkful in her mouth and closes her eyes, savoring the flavors. How is this woman eating?

I dip a tiny forkful of my fritter in the advertised caramel. As much as I hate to admit it, this tastes awesome.

"This is delicious! I wasn't expecting it to be this excellent. Do you want to try some?" I pick up my knife, cut her off a piece, and wave it under her nose.

"Sure," she says, leaning forward and taking it from me. "Mm, oh yeah, this is fantastic," she moans.

"Right? Good food is everything, isn't it, Marcy?"

"Indeed. And you have Joey as your personal chef. How lucky are you?" She raises her glass in a toast, and I do the same.

"I'm lucky," I agree.

Marcy and I steer clear of anything heavy for the rest of lunch. We laugh, we drink, comment on the hipster crowd around us, and for a while, I almost push the Bob and Marcy mess out of my mind.

Almost.

I hope I can forget about them altogether. At least the Bob part, anyway. As if. I wish I could wash my brain out with soap. All I want to do is go home and hug my husband.

But when Marcy eagerly tries to pin me down for lunch again a week from today, I say yes without hesitation.

Why? Maybe because I still need answers about Claude—and I can't pretend I'm not dying to know more

Five

I take an Uber home and try to digest everything Marcy said. Man, the part about Claude Bissonette completely blows my mind.

Dr. Bissonette wasn't my direct boss, just the president of the whole freaking museum. Something was terrifying about him. He was such an alpha male that I could feel myself shrinking in his presence. I probably only had ten more-than-a-few-seconds conversations with him the entire thirty years he was at the museum, but it's all such a blur right now, I can't recall anything.

I do, however, clearly remember the first time I met him as a new hire. I made a complete idiot of myself. I felt like I couldn't form a sentence. He asked my name. Instead of replying like a normal human being, I tried to be cute and responded, "Why?"

Fortunately, he laughed, but I still cringe at the memory, and to this day, I don't know "why" I said that. I was already happily married.

He turned my brain into mush.

But apparently, I wasn't alone. The entire staff was affected that way whenever he walked into the room. One of his many charismatic superpowers was the ability to tongue-tie a person.

You would have had to be an eunuch or made of ice not to be mesmerized by Dr. Claude Bissonette. Tall and thin with dark, wavy, windswept hair, high cheekbones, and heavily lashed light green eyes, he more resembled a male model on a romance novel clinch cover than a brilliant academic and art historian.

At one point, he even took to wearing a long black cape. He not only got away with it, but many of us copied him.

Hey, we thought he was the epitome of cool. And he was.

His wife was a former ballerina, I think. I'm not sure because I only met her once at a museum function many years ago. I remember she was tiny, blonde, and shockingly beautiful. We all gossiped afterward that she acted like royalty and we were the common folk. We had to admit we would expect nothing less in a spouse from Dr. Bissonette.

How in the world did he end up with Marcy?

How did they meet?

Was it me? Did I introduce them? How was that even possible? Wait. Did I ever invite Marcy to a museum function?

I have a faint, lingering memory of her showing up for lunch once, but I'm not sure.

I have so many questions.

But twenty years! How did frumpy, boring Marcy keep a man like Claude Bissonette interested?

I laugh to myself. Well, wait. She sure as hell isn't boring; I found that out at lunch today. I'm still reeling.

I have never thought of Marcy as attractive. But…maybe she was. I try to remember her at thirty years old. It was the eighties; everyone had long, permed curly hair. I think of Marcy back then; I conjure up an image and all I see is big hair and big tits.

Oh.

My thoughts race as the Uber makes the turn onto Penny Lane. Should I tell Joey everything Marcy shared at lunch? Or should I wait until I hear the entire story about Claude? I never know how Joey will react to stuff like this; he might get triggered.

However, how do I keep this to myself?

I shake my head. Nah, I should wait until I get the rest of the story.

I decide not to tell him. I don't want to upset him. Joey is, for the most part, mild-mannered and non-reactive except when it comes to people who have what he considers lapses in moral judgment. Despite being open-minded and a child of the sixties, he's not a fan of marital infidelity under any circumstances.

But there's a reason for that.

If a person could have the complete opposite childhood of mine, it would be Joey. He grew up living with Judy in dark, seedy apartments. He slept on a sofa bed and was constantly shuffled off to babysitters whenever Judy had a new boyfriend, which was often.

Judy's taste in men was dubious; she didn't know who Joey's father was. It could have been one of the twelve men she slept with the summer she graduated high school and took a waitress job at the Jersey shore.

She waited on tables her entire life until her death.

Despite working in restaurants, or maybe because of that, Judy never prepared any proper meals or kept much food (or anything nutritious) in their kitchen. Joey learned how to cook and be inventive as a young boy when he realized he would starve if he didn't.

Luckily, his general curiosity about the world and his vow to be nothing like his mother makes him an A student, resulting in a full college scholarship where he majored in culinary arts. I smile to myself, remembering Joey back in those days. He was just so adorable. I couldn't keep my hands off him.

I still can't.

The Uber driver interrupts my pleasant romp down memory lane.

"Oh man, look at that old crazy house. I bet the neighbors love that." He shoots me a snarky glance, then quickly retreats when he catches my expression. He doesn't know what to make of it. I resist the urge to slap him in the back of the head.

"Ah, so it's called Candyland," he quips, nodding toward the sign with a chuckle that lingers a little too long. He's amused until he glances at the address and makes the connection.

"Oh! This is your stop?" he stammers, his earlier humor replaced by nervous charm.

"Yeah," I shrug, fumbling with the seat belt. I don't know whether to laugh or be upset, it's been that kind of day.

He twists around again and stares at me beseechingly in the back seat. "It's really cool! I love old, funky houses. I didn't mean anything bad," he backpedals, eyes hopeful.

Sure you didn't.

I look at my phone and pull up the Uber app.

"It's okay, I know you aren't trashing my house," I smile. "It's fine. Really." I feel bad for him, he's young, cute, and driving an old lady in an Uber on a beautiful afternoon.

I tip him 25% and give him five stars.

Joey is watching television when I walk in the door. He jumps up to kiss me.

"Hey. Look at you! Survived an afternoon with Marcy Garber. See? I told you it wouldn't be that bad. You're here and still breathing, so at least she didn't bore you to death, right?" He stops when he sees my face. "Right?" he asks louder.

"Oh, she didn't bore me, that is for sure," I blurt out.

Joey looks sharply at me. "What's that supposed to mean?" He knows me so well.

"Nothing."

He raises his eyebrows and pressures me more. "That's not your 'nothing' face, Linda. What happened? Did Marcy tell you where the bodies are buried?" He stops when he sees my expression, which is a mix of reluctance and *ooh, ooh* I have something to tell you.

Hmmm...I wonder if he knows about Bob. Bob probably bragged to him. *Eww,* no, too gross. I'm not going there.

Joey arches his brows, a hint of worry etched across his face. "Hey, I was only kidding, Linda. Is everything okay? You seem pretty upset, and you're terrible at hiding your emotions."

I look down at my feet, unwilling to meet his glance, but he persists.

"Seriously, babe, what is it? What happened at lunch?"

Ugh, no. I don't want to tell him. What do I say? Think, Linda, think. Aha! How about nothing but the truth! Just not all of it.

"Oh, nothing happened. *Um*, other than Marcy flirted with the waiter who was young enough to be her grandchild. Then she ordered a cocktail called "Sex On A Beach", or something ridiculous like that, and I spent the whole time slumped in my seat, cringing."

I hope I don't get struck by lightning, but then again, I'm not lying. Just omitting.

Joey interrupts me with a big smile. "Grace and Frankie go to the wine bar," he interjects, laughing. "Which one are you, Jane Fonda or Lily Tomlin?"

"I think Marcy and I are both Lily," I say. "Not that there's anything wrong with Jane, but I still blame her for the exercise craze."

Well, it's true.

Joey laughs because he liked anti-war Jane better, too.

"I missed you while you were gone. I was reduced to watching a rerun of *The Golden Girls*," he remarks. He pulls me close and kisses me.

I rest my head against his chest and sigh.

"Wanna go upstairs?" he whispers, running his fingers up and down my spine.

"The *Golden Girls* makes you horny?" I tease, smiling. I rub up against him and kiss him back, even though all I want to do is lay down and take a nap.

But then, a fleeting vision of an extraordinarily handsome man with windswept hair, wearing a long black cape pops into my brain before I can stop it.

"Upstairs?" Joey asks again, releasing me from our hug.

"Okay," I purr, giving him my best smoky look. My husband is a very sexy man. Even without a cape.

I may be old, but I'm not dead yet.

Take that, Marcy Garber.

Oy.

Six

As it turns out, I can't meet Marcy for lunch again the following week after all. We got an unexpected call from Jazzy, letting us know she's going to be in New York doing a food and wine festival. Since Food Television is putting her up in a luxury dog-friendly Airbnb, do we want to bring Chester and visit for a few days?

You think?

We pack excitedly. Joey and I are giddy at the prospect of seeing our daughter and eating our way across Manhattan. Even though Joey professes to be underwhelmed by the whole celebrity chef food scene, all his reservations disappear when it comes to Jazz.

She's the star who can do no wrong, and I am just star-struck enough to agree.

Except when I don't.

Like the move to Seattle. I just can't let it go.

Oh man, why couldn't she have picked New York?

"She could have chosen Italy," Joey said to calm me down when she first announced her plans and told us about the amazing place she bought on Puget Sound.

"Italy? Well, at least I know we would have followed her there," I replied miserably.

Joey didn't respond, and at first, I thought he was going to change the subject. I know he probably hoped I would let it drop. Since I knew it would just start another argument about Candyland (that I wouldn't win), he was right. I stayed quiet.

It was Joey who didn't.

"We are not moving to Seattle," he said, scowling.

I looked down at my feet and willed the conversation to end. There was a lot I could say, but it wasn't the time.

Joey isn't finished.

He looks at me incredulously. "We have a history with our house. We raised a child here. Every room is crammed with memories. The mural you painted in the hallway. The growth chart we penciled on Jasmine's closet door. How can you even think of walking away from the home we made together? Can you imagine anyone else living here?"

I didn't say what I was thinking. No one else would want to live in this rundown old place. Whoever bought Candyland was going to knock it down and build three LEGO townhomes in its place.

I must admit that I felt so sad at the thought of our house being reduced to rubble that I ended up agreeing with Joey. Of course, we could never sell our house. Leaving Candyland was not an option. Even if it physically kills us taking care of it and it ends up eating our entire retirement savings.

Oy, I don't want to think about that.

I'm no psychiatrist, but I also figured that Joey's childhood was another factor in how he felt about our home and his need for roots and stability. I had a similar queasy vibe about moving. We bought Candyland with the money we got from selling my parents' home when we got married after college.

An art major like me and a line chef like Joey back then could never have afforded such a luxurious place. We used to walk from room to room in awe, holding a glass of wine in one hand and a joint in another.

"Do you believe we own this place?" Joey would ask.

"No, I don't. We are so freaking lucky," I always replied.

Oh, man. I can't imagine life without Candyland.

But I also can't imagine growing older alone in Philadelphia either, in a house way too much for anyone to take care of, let alone two stoner senior citizens. Worse, I worry that we'll drift farther away from our daughter. We spend almost every holiday and birthday just the two of us. Joey doesn't know it, but I always go off by myself and cry on those days.

Time is marching by. Things aren't going to get better as we age. Just the opposite. It's scary as fuck.

Is what Joey and I are doing now really living? Watching fifty-year-old reruns of *Match Game* and *Matlock*?

Oh my god, I sound like Marcy Garber. One lunch with Marcy and I'm questioning my entire existence. Please kill me now.

I summon up my weird version of Buddhism and force myself to be present.

Living in the future is as soul-crushing as living in the past—a recipe for anxiety or nostalgia-driven despair. I know this, but I'm not perfect.

It's a beautiful morning. Joey and I throw our suitcases in the trunk, strap Chester in his bucket seat, and get in the car. I'm so excited I can hardly bear it. Joey backs out of the driveway, and we're off to New York in joyous moods, singing along to Beatles music and munching on icy cold grapes we brought along for the ride. Chester hangs his cute beagle head out the window; passing truckers on I-95 smile at him.

It's moments like this that I wish I could freeze time again.

"I'm excited to see Jazz's Airbnb," I remark. I asked her to send a link, but she wants us to be surprised."

Joey smiled and shook his head. "It's weird to think of an Airbnb in Manhattan," he comments. "The term 'Airbnb' makes me think of one of those silver campers from 1950 that you attach to your car. You roll up to the campsite, crack open a beer, and put up the fire for the barbecue. Mm… barbecue." Joey smacks his lips and winks at me.

"Yeah, not quite. This silver camper is a penthouse with a hot tub and two fireplaces," I laugh. "Though I bet it has a kick-ass kitchen."

"Kitchen? I didn't come to New York to cook!" Joey protests, but he's smiling.

Of course, he's already picturing himself and Jazz in the kitchen making breakfast tomorrow morning like old times. I would bet the house on that.

Our GPS directs us to a tree-lined street right off Central Park. It's a magnificent pre-war building with its own private parking. Who even knew this place existed?

I text Jazz that we're here.

She texts us back with security codes to get in. No bulky keys and wonky door jams for my daughter.

Unlike my husband, I love technology. I wish we had this system for Candyland.

But even I have to giggle at the idea of a fancy computer system on a rotting door frame.

Jazz is so lovely she takes my breath away, so much so that I don't even notice the interior of the penthouse at first. She's dressed entirely in white and wearing her dark curly hair long and wild like a gypsy. She's all dimples and flashing big blue eyes.

"Mom, Dad, you gotta see this place. Let me give you the tour. Hi Chester, remember me? I'm your big sister," she croons, swooping him up in her arms. Chester, who usually plays hard to get, doesn't struggle to free himself. He snuggles into her and gives her a sloppy kiss across the face.

Everyone loves Jazz. Not even Chester is immune to her charms.

The penthouse is breathtaking. Exposed brick walls, an ultramodern open kitchen, and a claw-foot tub that makes my heart skip a beat. An ornate, curved staircase leads to a guest bedroom with its own fireplace and private terrace, complete with a hot tub.

Holy hell, this is nice. A few days of this luxury and I'm never going to go home, where I'm still brushing my teeth in the tub because Joey hasn't gotten around to fixing our upstairs bathroom sink.

I don't know; being here with our daughter just feels right.

"Why don't you guys unpack and chill for a few? I have to run out and do a quick interview for the festival. Do you want to meet me in an hour? I'll text you where I am as soon as I know myself," Jazz beams.

"Sounds good," Joey replies. He cocks his head at her, a look of concern on his face. "Are you okay? Do you need anything? You know me. I can never stop being your father."

Jazz grins and pecks him on the cheek. "I'm fine, Dad. I'm a big girl, but just in case, I have a bunch of assistants to ensure I don't get into trouble."

I look over at Joey, amused. Jazz has assistants. Why am I not surprised? Joey and I have been her slaves since the day she came out of the womb.

"How is it possible that we are both indentured servants and reduced to complete mush by this tiny, eight-pound, curly-haired creature?" I said to Joey at 3:00 a.m. during the first week we brought her home from the hospital.

Joey laughed tiredly and sank back into the pillows.

Little did we know it was just the beginning. But oh, it's been fun.

Jazz, glowing with excitement, practically bounces out of her shoes. "I'm so stoked! There's someone I want you to meet!" she gushes, her eyes sparkling with mischief. She pauses only to glance at her watch, an apologetic smile tugging at her lips.

"I hate to rush off just as you guys arrive, but I've got a quick gig to handle. Once that's done, we'll grab dinner. Deal?"

I look at Joey to see if he's picking up on anything, but his face is neutral.

My stomach tightens. Joey's expression stays neutral, but his tension is palpable. "Oh? Who?" I ask, trying to keep my voice steady. Jasmine's last boyfriend was a very married bass player in a notoriously raucous metal band, and Joey had nearly had a heart attack when he found out. Luckily, the relationship didn't last.

"You'll see," she teases. The mystery in her voice only adds to my unease. "It's nothing. But you might think so."

Oy. My stomach flutters nervously.

"I wonder who she's dating now," I murmur to Joey after Jazz leaves for her interview.

"I don't want to know," he moans.

"Well, we're going to find out. Be nice."

"I'm always nice," he insists with a grin.

"You are, I agree. This penthouse though…" I trail off, taking in the surrounding opulence. "It's hard to believe our child lives like this. I mean, it's not new to us; we saw her place in Seattle, but it's still crazy to see this scale of luxury. Especially for someone as young as Jazz."

Jazz's fame is fairly recent. Her career didn't catapult until five years ago when she was on *Top American Chef.*

Joey makes a face. "I wish she weren't so famous. There are a lot of weirdos out there. I worry."

"I know. Me, too. But the perks sure are sweet, huh," I say, waving my arm around the room. There are a couple of signed Warhol lithographs on the wall. How'd I miss that? They add an undeniable edge of sophistication.

Joey stretches and glances at his watch. "I'm going to grab a shave and change," he says, already moving toward the door.

Yeah, I want to get out of my sweats too. I'm feeling severely underdressed in this environment. I nod. "Okay, let's unpack and hopefully Jazz will text soon."

The sun streams in through the windows, and I catch myself looking out longingly. It doesn't feel right being indoors on a sunny day in New York City, even if we are in an incredible space. I open the sliding glass door and step out onto the terrace. What a ridiculously gorgeous view. Life feels so perfect right now, it scares me.

Seven

⌂

Jazz texts us to meet her for dinner at the Intrepid Museum.

"The Intrepid Museum?" Joey raises an eyebrow. "That sounds like something you'll love, Linda. I" just trying to wrap my brain around what it represents. A museum devoted to fortitude and fearlessness?" he laughs.

I'm shocked. "You dolt! It's the *USS Intrepid* Museum. The *Intrepid* was a World War II aircraft carrier." I look at him, see the mischievous grin, and immediately feel bad for taking him seriously.

"So, there's a restaurant there?" he asks.

"No, I don't think so. Let me Google what this dinner is, exactly. Hang on." I fish my phone out of my back pocket.

"Oh, listen to this, Joey." I squint and read him what I find on Google:

> *Hosted by award-winning TV personality and restaurateur Chaz Chipolata, this event brings pasta lovers together to take in the magnificent city skyline at Pier 86, home of The Intrepid Museum. Spend the night under the stars, with over twenty-five of New York City's finest pasta offerings.*

Joey looks relieved. "It sounds like we can wear jeans and T-shirts."

I'm still clicking on links and researching. "Oh, too funny. The pasta tasting is a competition. Chefs compete to win the Judge's Epicurean Award, voted on by a celebrity judge, Chaz Chipolata, and then there's a People's Choice Epicurean Award. Haha, here's your big chance to judge," I tease.

Joey pretends to gag.

"No thanks. But *ooh ooh*, we get to meet Chaz Chipolata," he remarks.

I laugh. I'm kind of excited about that. Joey, not so much. He's not a fan.

Chaz Chipolata and Food Television are synonymous. With cable television came Food Television, which launched its first hit show thirty years ago with a young, handsome chef named Chaz Chipolata, a self-anointed pasta king who loved the camera.

The camera loved him back. Chaz became an overnight star. Besides owning restaurants worldwide, he's now a corporate brand that sells everything from cookbooks to cat food.

His exploits with women are legendary. I'm pretty sure he's been married four or five times.

So he's got to be close to our age, but he's probably had some plastic surgery. Joey says he has hair plugs, but I can't tell. Honestly, I think he's cute.

Joey calls Chaz Chipolata a one-dimensional chef.

"Pasta. Who makes an entire career out of pasta?" he questions.

"I don't know, but I could make a career out of eating it," I say.

He gives me an exasperated look. Well, it's true. I could.

Joey is also no fan of Chaz's long-time show on Food Television. He competes against other chefs who all make the same dish and get judged blindly by a panel of three celebrity chefs. Chaz always wins.

"Oh, for Christ's sake," Joey scoffs, his tone dripping with exasperation. "Of course the judges know which dish is his. They're all chefs, for crying out loud. Chipolata has these signature moves—food riffs that are unmistakably his. He garnishes everything with pomegranate seeds, seasons with anchovies and black garlic, and acts like he invented these flavors. Somehow, he's made them his own. So, yeah, any talented chef worth their salt can tell it's his. It's like a guitarist hearing just one note and immediately recognizing Jimi Hendrix, or an art historian spotting a painting and instantly knowing the artist."

Joey leans back, his rant gaining momentum. "Chipolata thinks he's some kind of culinary Zorro, you know? Always leaving his mark—those telltale touches that scream his name. It's infuriating how he's turned his little bag of tricks into something revered, like he's pioneering a food revolution. But seriously, who does he think he's fooling? We all see through it."

"It's still gonna be cool to meet him," I remark.

"I'd rather meet Keith Richards," Joey fumes.

I shrug playfully. "Who wouldn't? If we lived in Seattle, Joey, we might have already partied with him last month."

But oh well, we're meeting Jazz and Chaz." I laugh at my comment. "Hey, look at that! I made a rhyme. Jazz and Chaz."

Joey is not amused. "Anyway, enough," I continue, noticing his lack of enthusiasm. "We could stand here all day, talking about should have, would have, could have, and I don't want to waste another minute of our time in New York doing that. We both know better. It's almost time to meet up with Jazzy. We need to get changed and order an Uber. It's too far to walk."

"It better not be Jazz and Chaz," Joey grumbles.

Oh, great.

"*Eww*, no, he's our age, Joey," I attempt to reassure him.

That comment does little to calm my husband; it infuriates him more. "And?" Joey growls. "You don't think these creepy rich guys date beautiful young women like our daughter?"

A knot forms in my stomach, tightening with each passing moment. "I just don't see Jazz dating him; she's picky." I cross my fingers, hoping he doesn't remember the married metal head bassist.

"Stop worrying. You realize we just created this whole scenario, right? All I did was Google where we're eating tonight and I saw Chaz Chipolata is hosting the event. For all we know, he and Jazz are practically strangers. He's probably dating some high-profile actress; that's his usual M.O."

Joey takes a deep breath and smiles. "You're right. I don't know why I got so crazy. She did say she wants us to meet someone, though."

"She did, but it could be anyone." A grin spreads across my face. "I'm excited. This is going to be fun. I'm looking at tonight as something cool that most people don't get to experience. Bob and Marcy Garber would kill to be here."

Joey laughs. "You and the Garbers. Ever since you had lunch with Marcy last week, you keep bringing them up. I think Marcy is your new bestie."

"Oy, no thanks. You, Jazz, and Chester are all the besties I need."

But I'm already thinking how I can't wait to tell Marcy all about this. I know it's weird, and I really don't want to analyze it, but I think her affair with my boss raises her status in my eyes.

Eight

The pier is set up like a carnival for the festival. There are twinkling lights everywhere and brightly colored vendor booths, each claiming to have the best award-winning pasta. Live music throbs through speakers. It's such a vibrant, eclectic mix of celebrities, foodies, and tourists, it's crazy. I laugh when I see a couple of hipsters wearing fedoras walking by eating fried ravioli on a stick.

Joey laughs too when he sees them. "What the actual fuck?"

"I wondered how they'd make pasta portable for this event," I giggle.

Joey looks so adorable; he has his indignant face on. "I think I would have come up with something more creative than a ravioli corn dog." He shakes his head once more, then asks, "Hey, did Jazz answer your text?"

"She's answering now," I mumble under my breath as I squint to see the words on my phone. "Oy, I think I need reading glasses. When it's dusk, I really struggle seeing. This getting older stuff sucks,"

I squint at the small screen until I can finally focus. "Oh, okay, Jazz is at Booth 50. The Pasta King. We're only at Booth 2. It must be at the end of this walkway here, closer to the water."

Joey sucks in his breath. "The Pasta King?"

"Yeah."

"Chaz Chipolata's flagship restaurant on Times Square," he snorts. "Hardly the best pasta."

"Well, duh, Joey. The best pasta is at our house," I say truthfully.

It's a beautiful spring evening. The air is fragrant with the wonderful unlikely combination of garlic and cherry blossoms as Joey and I push through the throngs of people sampling the food and wine. I stop to snap a few photos.

I shrug when I see Joey watching me. "Well, you know I have to take some pics for Marcy Garber," I explain.

"I love how you call her Marcy Garber, never just Marcy," Joey remarks with a smile.

"Ha, yeah, I think I like the way it sounds. Marcy Garber, Marcy Garber, Marcy Garber."

Joey takes my hand and squeezes it. "You're so fucking nuts. Please don't ever change."

I give him a little squeeze back. "No fucking chance."

Oh, how I love this man.

We both see Booth 50 at the same time. Set apart from the other booths and perched dramatically on the waterfront, it looms like a carnival king's palace, twice the size of its neighbors. A huge, spinning electronic billboard screams for attention, emblazoned with the chiseled face of Chaz Chipolata wearing a gigantic golden crown made from what looks like dried macaroni and basil leaves. The whole thing gleams in the twilight, a caricature of culinary royalty.

"Oh my god!" This is a whole new level of hilarious. It's like seeing a used car salesman dressed up like Julius Caesar. I can't help it. I laugh like an idiot.

"Yeah," Joey agrees, laughing along with me. "It's a little much."

Jazz is inside the booth, standing next to steam table pans of food. She's signing autographs, and there's an excited line of people calling out her name.

"Look, there's Chef Jazz! Chef Jazz! Chef Jazz! Can I get a picture with you?"

Joey and I stand off to the side, taking it all in. It's surreal, but our daughter really is a star.

I try to get her attention by walking back and forth and waving. Joey almost pees himself laughing.

Finally, she looks up and sees us. She puts down her pen and comes running out, blowing kisses.

"Mom! Dad! You found me! Isn't this insane? So much crazy delicious food! Did you have anything to eat yet? Dad, they just put out some *cacio e pepe*." She lowers her voice. "It's not as good as yours, but people go nuts over it. The secret is they add egg yolks."

"Egg yolks? So, it's carbonara then." Joey shrugs. "Not that I'm a stickler about food or anything."

Jazz laughs. "Well, you know, Dad, Chaz likes to put his spin on things."

Joey and I exchange looks.

Uh oh.

I look up at the neon flashing billboard of the Pasta King with the macaroni crown and then back at my young, gorgeous daughter.

Nah. No way. She'd never be attracted to someone like that.

But then I remember Marcy Garber and Claude Bissonette.

What do I know about anything anymore? But before I can sink too deeply into my thoughts, Jazz's cheerful voice breaks through, brimming with excitement.

"Mom, Dad," she says, practically bouncing with enthusiasm. "I'm sure you know who this is, but meet Chaz Chipolata. I've been dying to introduce you! Chaz, meet my parents, Joey and Linda Lisser."

And there he is, right in front of us, hair plugs, spray tan, golden macaroni crown and all. The Pasta King himself.

I wish I could take a picture of Joey's face. He looks like he just ate a bug.

"Hey, how's it going? Linda, Joey, you can't be the parents, you gotta be the siblings." He beams at us like he's the first person to have ever used that bullshit line, but who are we to disagree?

I beam right back at him for a second or two until I feel Joey's elbow jabbing me in the ribs. I give him a sideways look. His body language is stiff and unfamiliar. His facial expression is a cross between furious and homicidal.

Chaz is completely oblivious and continues with his spiel. "Fantastic girl you raised. She's going to be a major star. A major, major star," he gushes.

Jazz blushes. "Chaz is mentoring me at Food Television. There's been so much to learn. Cooking is the only simple part. You have to be "on" all the time, and I don't know if I'm that person."

"You're doing great," Chaz gushes. "I wish I had half your skills at your age." And then he turns to us. "Kids," he remarks, shrugging. "I've got a few of my own. If anyone ever learns the right way to deal with them, please let me know." Chaz winks at Joey and me with an impish grin.

There's something so genuine about his comment, I instantly exonerate him. I glance over at Joey, feeling a lot better. I believe the innocent, mentoring explanation for their relationship because I don't see any sexual tension between them, thank freaking god.

Joey is smiling. He's more relaxed, too.
Whew.

"Hey, it was nice meeting you guys, but I have to run," Chaz says, looking at his phone. "My assistant claims this competition 'isn't going to judge itself.' Okay then, The Pasta King is on his way." Chaz waves at us before scampering away. "Sorry we didn't have more time to chat, folks. If we don't meet again, enjoy the rest of your trip. Ciao!"

And just like that, he disappears into the crowd.

Jazz looks relieved. Even better.

She tosses her lovely dark curls. "I am starving. Let the pasta party begin!"

It's like old times. The three of us walk from booth to booth, stuffing our faces and giving hilarious blow-by-blow commentary on the food. We taste gnocchi in brown butter, gnudi with fried sage, roasted squash ravioli, and pesto pasta with potatoes and green beans. And that's just the appetizers.

All evening, people call out her name. Jazz graciously smiles and waves while we positively gush by her side.

"It's like she's running for president," I whisper to Joey.

"That's next year," he smiles.

The wine is flowing everywhere, and we don't exactly drink responsibly. Who cares? We're together, and nobody's driving. We laugh until we are out of breath and collapse on a nearby bench.

I wish we could do this every night.

I'm intoxicated with not just the wine but the fragrant spring night, the perfect food, and the magical presence of our daughter.

For at least the second time today, I wish I could freeze time.

Nine

❤

Joey and I wake up the next morning, so hungover we want to die. Adding to our pain, a windy, pouring rain is pounding hard against the floor-to-ceiling windows in the penthouse. New York City looks bleak and colorless below.

Jazz, however, is a vision in turquoise and coral, sitting on the oversized sofa, sipping coffee.

"Good morning!" she calls out cheerfully.

"*Ugh*, is it?" I try not to hiss.

Jazz chuckles, her voice light and teasing. "Can't hold your liquor anymore, Mom?"

Joey, lounging in the background, chimes in with a grin, "When could Mom ever hold her liquor?"

Their laughter fills the room as I groan dramatically, clapping my hands over my ears. The gesture only fuels their amusement, their laughter ringing even louder.

Breaking the moment, I shift my focus to the day ahead. "So, what's the plan for today?" I ask, my voice carrying a note of hope as I wander to the sliding glass door. The rain beats relentlessly against the sidewalk outside, a steady rhythm against the glass. "Please tell me it doesn't involve anything outdoors?"

"Nah, everything is inside the Intrepid. I'm hosting a burger bash at noon and a taco and tequila party at three o'clock." She wrinkles her nose. "This is all corny tourist bullshit and so totally not your thing, but the money goes to charity so there's that.

"Do you guys want to come, or do you want to hang here in ze penthouse until I'm finished?"

"I vote for the Penthouse," says Joey.

"Me, too," I agree.

Jazz flashes us a triumphant look. "*Ha*, I figured that. I know you both so well. Anyway, I'm free around five, as soon as I'm done slinging tacos. Mom, for dinner there's an insane vegetarian Asian fusion place I've been dying to take you, and Dad to. Trust me, you'll love it. Just don't wear socks with holes in them," she laughs.

I shake my head to clear the brain fog. "Huh?"

"It means we're taking our shoes off for dinner," Joey explains.

I smile happily. "Oh".

Jazz walks into the kitchen and rinses out her cup.

"Okay, I'm taking off. If you change your mind and want to meet up, shoot me a text. And if you get hungry, take a look at this," she instructs, opening the refrigerator.

"Oh my god, it's a mini Whole Foods," I blurt out in surprise. But my hungover stomach suddenly objects, and I have to look away.

"But I'll be back for you later," I whisper to the fruit salad.

Jazz puts on a raincoat, grabs an umbrella, and walks out the door. Thunder rumbles in the distance; the apartment grows darker.

"Oh, man, it's just like when she was a little girl," I remark to Joey. "When Jazz is in the room, everything turns to rainbows, but when she leaves, it goes all black and white. No, make that gray."

Joey grins and nods. "Truth."

Neither one of us has to state the obvious, but I sure as hell am thinking it in terms of our life since she moved to Seattle.

"What should we do, go back to bed, take a soak in the hot tub, or what?" Joey asks. "How are you feeling? Any better? Do you want anything to eat?"

"I'm feeling better. Hot tub and bed, please. Or bed and hot tub, you decide," I remark, kissing him.

"Okay," he murmurs, pulling me close.

Joey kisses me over and over as we walk up the magnificent staircase to our bedroom. We rip off our clothes like teenagers and make love under a Warhol silkscreen of Marilyn Monroe, on top of Charlotte Thomas Bespoke bed sheets that have twenty-four karat gold woven directly into the fabric and cost more than our entire set of bedroom furniture at home. I know this only because I read in *People* magazine that the Kardashians sleep on them, and somehow this made it into my bank of useless knowledge.

For once, Chester behaves himself and doesn't try to join in. Usually, we have to lock him out, and he scratches the door and howls like someone is trying to kill him. Today he is the perfect little prince, snoring gently and contentedly in the far corner of our king-size bed.

We fall into a deep sleep, wake up in the early afternoon, soak in the hot tub, and make love again.

"Not bad for two people in their sixties," Joey whispers.

"We're so lucky," I smile.

However, after that, we're so wiped out that we nap the rest of the day, except for bathroom breaks and five minutes of standing at the refrigerator eating fruit salad right out of the container with two forks.

Jazz texts at 6:00 to meet her for dinner, waking us both from a sound sleep.

"Jesus Christ, I could have slept until tomorrow," Joey splutters, struggling into his jeans.

"Me, too," I agree. "If I didn't have the ringer turned up on my phone, we probably would have. Meanwhile, what's this about socks? I didn't even bring any. Do you have extras?"

Joey opens the dresser and tosses me a pair. "My last clean ones."

"Really? I know we're supposed to stay until Thursday, but I'm just as happy to go home tomorrow. I can only take New York in small doses and god knows what Jazz has planned for us tonight," I remark. "I'm just happy I don't have to do it in my bare feet."

Jazz tells us to meet her a few blocks away at what I can only call an oasis. Google describes it as the Narnia of Koreatown. We take off our shoes and sit on soft, luxurious cushions at low teak wood tables. Our server brings us a gorgeous porcelain teapot and pours us a cup as he recites the specials.

The menu is magnificent. There's crispy batter sweet potato, kabocha pumpkin, taro, broccoli, beet and onion patties, minced oyster mushrooms

71

and tofu wrapped in sesame leaves, and Korean sweet potato noodles with assorted vegetables.

We order it all, along with two bottles of sake. Jazz puts her arm around me and kisses my cheek.

This may be the best day of my life.

The waiter brings our sake and we hold up our cups to toast.

"To the three musketeers. May we live long and prosper," s.

We clink glasses and drink.

"So, Mom, Dad, I judged the burger bash today, and too funny, the winner was from a hipster bar in Philadelphia."

"Oh yeah? Which bar?" I ask.

"Eh, I forget. But I remember the name of their winning dish—it's a 'face bacon' burger," she remarks, rolling her eyes.

"What the actual fuck is a face bacon burger?" Joey asks, pouring us all another drink.

"Nose-to-tail bacon," Jazz says with a laugh.

"Wait, isn't all bacon nose to tail?" I ask with a disdainful tone.

Jazz and Joey laugh at me.

"So basically, it's guanciale," Joey explains.

"Whatever. It's gross." I stick my tongue out at them.

We kill off the first bottle of sake before our meals are even on the table. When it arrives, Jazz is right, the food is a showstopper. It's while we're drinking the second bottle, I realize I can't feel my feet and am about to get the charley horse from hell.

Whoever thought it was a good idea for a woman in her sixties to eat dinner sitting on a pillow on the hard, hard ground?

Hey, at least I am providing a floor show for my husband and daughter. They're laughing so hard at my attempt to stand on two feet that are completely asleep that I may have to kill them.

But I have to laugh too because it's hilarious. I limp to the ladies' room to get blood circulating.

What a night. How I love my family. But once again, there was too much eating and drinking. I wake up in the middle of the night parched; there's no way in hell I can sleep. Joey and Chester snore in unison and don't even hear me get out of bed.

As I tiptoe down the fancy staircase, the silence feels heavy, pressing against my skin like the storm outside. In the dim lighting, the apartment suddenly seems less familiar, and a sense of unease settles over me as I sip icy-cold spring water in the dark kitchen.

When the door to Jazz's bedroom cracks open, the chill in my spine confirms that something isn't right. *Oh no, I hope I didn't wake her.* I open my mouth and start to call out to her, but a second later, I freeze.

It isn't Jazz.

What the hell? Who is that?

Suddenly, my dinner threatens to revisit my lips, thanks to the sake and the sight of the person in the doorway. *Oh, my god!*

It's Chaz Chipolata.

I press up against the wall, horrified. Hopefully, he doesn't see me. I'm willing myself to be invisible.

Chaz walks toward the door, but just as I'm almost collapsing with relief, he stops dead in his tracks. My breath catches, and my heart pounds so loudly I'm certain he can hear it. Chaz stands frozen, shrouded in darkness, and time stretches unbearably. When his face suddenly lights up, I nearly scream—but then I see it. The soft glow of his phone. He's checking a text.

For a moment, his features resemble a devil from a nightmare, the shadows dancing malevolently across his face. My legs threaten to give out, but I cling to stillness. Then, without a word, he slips his phone into his pocket and disappears through the door.

It's only after the faint click of the latch that I let out a shaky exhale and force myself to drain my bottle of water. *No. No way am I telling Joey about this. Never.*

I tiptoe back upstairs. Joey and Chester are exactly as I left them. They don't even know I was gone; that gives me a sad brief pang.

I snuggle into the luxury bedding and tell myself not to have any disgusting thoughts. It works. Somehow, I fall asleep.

The next morning, we have coffee with Jazz before she heads back to the food and wine festival and we head back to Philadelphia.

I stare at her and will her to read my mind.

THE PASTA KING? OH MY GOD, WHAT ARE YOU THINKING?

She happily sips her coffee and chatters, with no idea what insanity is going through my head and I stay quiet. Until Joey excuses himself to go to the bathroom and shower.

"I got up at three in the morning to get a glass of water," I mumble, looking into her eyes.

She tosses her curls. "Oh?"

"I don't know how else to say this, but *eww*, Jazz. Just…*eww*." I don't have to fake a gag, I do it.

"Mom. I'm over thirty years old."

"I know that, but Jazz, he's almost my age! What could you possibly have in common?"

Jazz grins at me over the rim of her coffee cup. "Sex?"

My mouth opens and closes like a dying fish gasping for air. "Oy vey," I reply weakly, without thinking. Hey, at least I didn't say *eww* again, which is my true and guttural response.

"Mom, do you know how hard it is to find a good sexual partner? Either they can't get it up or they don't last more than two seconds. You find someone like Chaz, you hold on to him."

She smirks and tosses her curls rebelliously. "I just realized you've been with Dad your whole life; you have no idea what I'm talking about or what it's like out there."

"I know what it's like out there," I reply defensively. But really, I'm speechless. Jazz is right. I have no clue, thank god.

Jazz laughs. "Mom, I don't love Chaz. I like him and he's great for my career. Men have been using women for years. Chaz is not my forever man, trust me."

"Okay, cool," I murmur weakly.

"Hey, ladies! What did I miss?" Joey walks in, fresh from the shower, smiling from ear to ear.

"Not a thing," Jazz replies, staring at me.

"Nothing at all," I agree, avoiding her gaze. There are some things Joey is better off not knowing.

Ten

⌂

I meet Marcy for lunch at Terroir again, calling it "our place" when she reminded me was my turn to pick the restaurant. The food is outstanding. I like both the intimate ambiance and our waiter, Sean, who comes sprinting when he sees us (he even remembers our drink order). He's so cute.

"So how was New York?" Marcy asks before I unfold my napkin and place it in my lap.

I smile and settle back in my chair. "So much fun!" I reply.

During the Uber ride to the restaurant, I debated telling Marcy about Jazz and Chaz. *Ugh*, Jazz and Chaz. Somehow, I no longer find the rhyming names funny; in fact, they make me extremely nauseous. But ultimately, I decide not to. It's bad enough I didn't tell Joey about it, nor did I tell him about Bob's womanizing, or Marcy's affair with my boss.

Until last week, I never kept anything from Joey. We tell each other everything.

Now I feel like I'm a CIA double agent or something, and it's making me crazy. I'm not good with secrets. I like talking stuff out, especially with Joey. I've been feeling woozy for the past couple of days because I've stressed out about this whole thing. "How's Jazz? Did you guys meet anyone famous in New York?" Marcy interrupts my train of thought, but so does Sean, who arrives with the breadbasket and our drinks.

I grab a piece of focaccia studded with rosemary. Sean pours olive oil into a pretty porcelain dish and I dip my bread in hungrily.

"Damn, this is good," I say, chewing and talking with my mouth full. Who cares if I'm eating like a slob, there's got to be some perks to getting older.

I used to think that getting older would come with the perk of finally being comfortable in my skin—a nice little reward for surviving life's ups and downs. But that's the thing about life: it loves a good joke, and I'm the punchline.

The older I get, the more I feel like I'm regressing. It's not just the hair thinning or the wrinkles sneaking up like uninvited guests; it's the sudden, sharp realization that time doesn't just age you—it strips away the illusion of control. The parallels with childhood are impossible to ignore.

First, you rely on others to help you navigate the world; then you fight like hell for your independence. And just when you think you've got it all figured out, life starts to tiptoe back toward dependency. It's terrifying. And that's not even touching the thoughts of mortality—the creeping worry about dying alone. So I never let my mind go there.

Except when it does. Marcy put the seedlings of death thoughts in my brain the last time we had lunch. I thought I quashed them; apparently not.

The other day I was sitting on the sofa and a patch of sunlight lit up my exposed skin. What I saw caused me to recoil in horror.

"Oh my god, Joey. Look at these wrinkles. My arm looks like the Declaration of Independence!" I exclaimed, completely freaked out.

Joey looked up from the television, confused. "Huh? The Declaration of what now?"

I shoved my elbow under his nose. "My skin looks like two hundred fifty-year-old parchment paper. Oy. I'm so old."

Joey gave me an annoyed look and pushed my arm away. "Oh for fuck's sake, you're not old," he said. "And, if you are, it sure beats the alternative."

"The alternative to what, being young and beautiful?" I smiled even though inside, I was a quivering mass of goo.

When did this happen? Wasn't I just congratulating myself on how good I looked?

It's weird watching things slowly decompose. First Candyland, now me.

"Linda? Earth to Linda? Did you hear me? I agree with you about the bread, it's fantastic. I want to dump the entire basket in my handbag and take it home for dinner," Marcy admits, bringing me back to the present. "But come on, I want to hear all about New York! Who did you get to meet at the food and wine festival?"

"Oh, we only met Chaz Chipolata," I remark offhandedly, trying to ignore the taste of rosemary suddenly turning to ashes.

Marcy blinks, then suddenly morphs into a squealing teeny bopper. It's not pretty. "The Pasta King? You met the Pasta King? Oh my god, I'm freaking out. I love him! Chaz is so dreamy, I would have lost my mind. What's he like in person?"

For a moment I'm tempted to say, "How about I introduce the two of you? He's no Claude Bissonette but if you can keep him occupied so he keeps his old man hands off my sweet young daughter, I would appreciate it very much, thank you" but I take a long, long sip of my drink.

"Chaz's very charming," I say carefully after a few seconds. "Jazz seems to like him. He's offered to mentor her at Food Television. He's firm that she's a star."

Marcy smiles. "We've known that since she was born."

"Aw, thanks, Marcy." I study the menu, gripping its sides as if that will help calm me. The thought of Chaz makes me a candidate for an antacid commercial. "Hey Marcy, do you know what you're having?" I ask, hoping to change the subject.

"Honestly, the shrimp were so good, I've been dreaming about them, so I'm going with that. What are you getting?"

"The spicy dan dan noodles with black vinegar-glazed trumpet mushrooms. That's right up my alley," I tell her.

Marcy laughs. "I can't believe you're a vegetarian with such talented chefs in the family. How does Joey feel about that?"

"Well, I've been a vegetarian for years, so he's used to it. He claims it made him up his cooking game." Okay, Joey laughed at me when I told him I was giving up meat, but when he realized it was permanent, he understood and rose to making vegetables the star of my meals.

"Joey is incredible," she sighs.

"Indeed," I reply.

Marcy leans closer and raises her eyebrow. "So, what else did you guys do in New York? Did you meet anyone else famous? You know I live vicariously through you," she giggles.

She does? *I'm not the one with the twenty-year affair with your boss, Marcy.*

I tilt my glass slightly, watching how the light catches the liquid inside of it. "Nah, we didn't meet any other celebrities. The first night, Monday, we went to a pasta festival and ate and drank like pigs."

"Is that where you met Chaz?" Marcy asks excitedly. She licks her top lip, as if she's tasting him. It's all I can do not to shudder.

"On Tuesday it rained sideways, and we had such hangovers we decided to stay in and enjoy Jazz's penthouse and hot tub while she did cooking demonstrations at the food and wine festival," I continued. "Though we met her for dinner at this amazing Asian fusion place. We also drank a couple of bottles of sake."

"That sounds like fun to me! Man, you guys are so lucky. I'd kill to spend just a few days in your shoes," Marcy sighs. "So, then what?"

"We'd had our fill of spicy food, drinks, and the hot tub by Wednesday; it was enough for a lifetime, so we decided to return home a day early."

Marcy sinks back in her chair, disappointed. Should I have lied and told her I partied with the cast of *Saturday Night Live* just to get her reaction? Just as I begin to fantasize about it, Sean materializes to take our order. This time we're smart enough to ask for a second round of drinks before we finish the first, in case he disappears again.

I need to relax and not think about Jazz and Chaz.

"So, what's new with you, Marcy? Did you do anything interesting while Joey and I were in New York?" I hate making stilted conversation; it makes me like some pretentious bitch talking to the bagger boy at a supermarket. Especially when all I want to ask is, "So, when did you start fucking my boss, Marcy?"

"*Meh*, there's nothing new." Then Marcy perks up. "But one interesting development, I told my therapist about Belize, and she's all for it! I never expected that in a million years. Honestly, I got the vibe she's considering it herself."

I lift my head and stare at her. Belize? Huh? What did I miss here?

"Belize?"

"Oh, I didn't tell you about that? Bob and I are talking about moving there."

I stare at her, not knowing what to think or feel. "Wait, what? Why Belize?" I search my brain. Where the heck is it? Central America?

Marcy beams. "Well, for one thing, there's a large group of expats living there. I've been corresponding with a few women, and they tell me it's nirvana, a beautiful country where it's summer all year round. There's a low cost of living and a no-frills kind of lifestyle. Bob and I could live in a waterfront place on a fabulous beach for less than we pay a month for our crummy fifty-year-old apartment that doesn't even have a washer/dryer in the unit."

"You don't have a washer/dryer?" I'm so shocked I blurt it out without thinking.

Marcy sighs. "No, I don't. How sad is that? So yeah, I don't want to be eighty years old, dragging a laundry basket up and down the scary cellar steps."

She sighs and fidgets with her glass. "As it is, I live in fear that the landlords will sell our building and knock it down for a high rise. They're elderly, but their son is the manager. I feel like he's just waiting for them to die so he can cash in. Can you imagine if that happens? Where would we go? We have zero savings. Everything is so expensive now; we're never going to find another decent apartment in Philadelphia. And if god forbid Bob dies, how will I even be able to afford food living where we do now?"

I slam my hand on the table. "Oh my god, Marcy. If Bob dies? Don't say that!" It's like she's been reading my mind lately. Or do all people our age obsess about death?

I'm rattled because I'm triggered. Death is something I have worked hard over the years not to think about or let it guide my decisions. Yet here it is, the topic of choice for seniors everywhere; there's no escape. But Marcy doesn't know how I feel, or if she does, she doesn't care.

Marcy looks at me pityingly. "Oh, Linda. You can't run from death. Death is life. The only question is, what would you do, how do you go on? If Bob dies tomorrow, I would be on a plane to Belize the next day. You would do the same."

I smile weakly. "I would go to Belize the day after Bob died?"

Marcy frowns and folds, then refolds her napkin. It's obvious she's annoyed with me. "Very funny. Nah, you know what I mean. If anything happens to Joey, wouldn't you move to Seattle? And if god forbid something happens to you, don't you think he would do the same?"

No. Maybe. Yes.

"I honestly never thought about it," I tell her truthfully.

"*Gah!*" she splutters, with a slightly crazed look in her eyes. "I think about it every damn day. Death happens all the time at our age. Have you looked at our alumni newsletter lately? Our *In Memoriam* section is six pages long. It's not an if anymore, it's a when."

"Six pages of our classmates are dead?" I stare at her with my mouth hanging open. "You're exaggerating, Marcy, or are there just two obituaries on the page? Please tell me you're kidding," I plead.

"I wish I were. Try one hundred per page. I read them all, some of them twice. I try not to dwell on it, but it does make you paranoid. Sometimes I get a crazy sharp pain somewhere, and I wonder, is this gas or a heart attack? What are the signs of a stroke? I think I'm having one. I want to ignore it all and not be a hypochondriac, but what if I die because I don't call an ambulance? I try not to, I really do, but I think about dying all the time."

Marcy pauses for dramatic effect. "And then," she continues, "I look over at Bob and I think he doesn't look good, he looks all pale and grayish and I worry so much. What if he's sick, and he's not telling me? Or what if he's not sick to his knowledge, but he has a sudden fatal heart attack or stroke? I don't want him to die and, by the same token, I'm not ready to die yet, either." Marcy wipes away a tear with the back of her hand.

"I hear you," I offer weakly. I'm not sure what else to say, other than *Please don't make me think about this, too, Marcy.*

"I just don't want to waste time worrying, and it seems like it's all I do these days," Marcy continues. "Belize represents a viable second chance for Bob and me. There's such a large community of happy retirees there, and it's better to do it now—before one of us gets sick, before it's too late."

She pauses briefly, her voice softening. "We can do the impossible at our age, we can start over. But this time, there will be no expectations of having fame or fortune. How liberating is that? And maybe…just maybe…we can salvage our lives in a magnificent place, a beach known for its magnificent coral reefs, etc., etc." She trails off, looking so wistful my heart hurts for her.

"Wow, when you put it that way, Marcy, jeez."

She's got my head spinning.

Marcy sniffles and searches her purse for a tissue. "Yeah. Sorry, I know I'm rambling, but I feel so strongly about this. All I have to do now is convince Bob. But he's coming around. He's probably sick of hearing me go on and on about it. If you and Joey ever move to Seattle, that'll seal the deal. We will have nobody left in Philadelphia."

I laugh. "I would love to help you. You need to talk to Joey. I would be in Seattle tomorrow if I could."

Sean arrives with our food and drinks. We make the appropriate fuss when he sets it down and beams at us.

"Oh my god, these shrimp," Marcy moans, closing her eyes and fanning herself.

"Enjoy, ladies," Sean says. I avert my eyes, bracing myself in case Marcy does something else ridiculous—like attempting to slip a ten-dollar bill down his pants.

My meal is delicious. The noodles are just as good, if not better, than anything I had last week in New York.

Sean appears table-side with a magical-looking tray. I could walk right past Tiffany's window and not give it a second glance, but this plate I want to kidnap and marry.

"You ladies look like you want to taste the best dessert you will ever have in your lifetime. Can I interest you in a salted caramel pistachio budino with cardamom cream and dark chocolate bark? Or a piquant tropical cheesecake with grilled pineapple, hibiscus jam, and tepache ice cream perhaps?"

"Yes!" we shout simultaneously.

I suspect Sean has been listening to our conversation and enjoying it. I think we broke the boring old lady stereotype for him.

I hope so.

"Do you want both, or do you want to pick one and share?" Sean asks, clearly pleased.

"Both! We want both!" Marcy replies without even checking with me; she already knows the answer. She leans forward and whispers, "What the hell is tepache ice cream?"

"Damned if I know," I whisper back.

"It's fermented pineapple," Sean answers, grinning.

"I should know that. My husband is a chef," I admit, blushing.

Sean cocks his head with an interested expression.

"Oh? Anyone I know? What's his name?"

He's retired," Marcy interrupts before I can reply. She smiles and continues, her voice loud enough for everyone in the restaurant to hear. "But I bet you know their daughter. She's Chef Jazz from Food Television!"

I turn about fifty shades of red and look down as everyone in the restaurant, it seems, turns to look at me.

Sean is startled. Is it my imagination or is he blushing? That, and he's flustered. I'm getting a real kick out of this.

"Chef Jazz is your daughter? I love her, she's so, so great. Wow! What a coincidence. I'm a server for Chef Jazz's mother."

I stifle a grin. Sean's lost his cool and is gushing all over the place.

The people at the next table stare and smile at me.

"Yep, I'm the proud mom," I blush.

Sean is still incredulous; he's practically hopping from foot to foot. "That's incredible. I

87

watched her season on *Top American Chef* and rooted for her to win. And then I met her at a chefs' event. We have her poster hanging in the kitchen. Wait until I tell the rest of the staff. Chef Jazz's mom. Hey, listen, desserts are on me today. You guys are royalty. Be right back with your order."

I cock my head to the side and eye him curiously. "You're a chef?"

Sean reddens. "Yeah," he mumbles.

Marcy squints at Sean and cuts straight to the point. "You're a chef, and now you're waiting tables? What happened?"

I groan inwardly, wishing I could vanish into thin air. *Please kill me now.* Marcy has no shame. She's about as subtle as a brick to the face.

"The pandemic…the pandemic happened," Sean says solemnly.

But then he flashes us a thousand-watt smile. He seems cool with everything.

"No worries. I still cook nights at my buddy's bar in Fishtown. I only wait tables here at lunchtime a few days a week to pay off some debt sooner rather than later."

Sean pauses, his smile never wavering. "Anyway, enough about me. Let me get you those desserts." He turns on his heel and heads toward the kitchen.

"You should fix Sean up with Jazzy. He's so cute. Let's find out if he has a girlfriend," Marcy insists as he walks away.

"How do we know he isn't gay?" I ask her, even though I'm pretty positive he isn't.

Marcy blushes. "Oh! I hadn't thought of that. I can never tell. I have zero gaydar." Good. Maybe she'll leave Sean alone.

I almost tell her about Chaz Chipolata right here and now, but honestly, I've had enough squealing for today.

Sean brings us dessert, and it's amazing. I am so into it and so woozy from the cocktails that it isn't until I'm on the way home that I realize I never asked Marcy anything else about Claude Bissonette.

Eleven

The mailman brings us a letter with a picture of our house on the envelope. I rip it open and start laughing.

"Listen to this, Joey. Stone Investment Properties wants to buy Candyland. They show us other comparable homes in the neighborhood that sold for two million dollars and more," I say.

"What? Let me see that," Joey exclaims, holding out his hand. I pass the letter over to him and watch, interested, as he reads. After a few seconds, he makes a face, crumbles it up, and tosses it in the trash. I make a mental note to retrieve it later. Because just in case.

Joey scowls. "Yeah, they're not talking about Candyland for that price. So the LEGO houses are going for two million? They're…they're row houses, for fuck's sake. Okay, row houses with Viking appliances and roof decks, but still. For two million dollars, I want a place on five acres with a lake." He slams his hand angrily on the table for emphasis.

I'm a bit taken aback at his uncharacteristic temper, but I agree with him about the ridiculous prices. Though secretly, my heart races at the thought of our run-down little property soon being worth enough money for us to move to Seattle.

"We're not selling Candyland, Linda." I open my mouth and shut it. It's as if the man can read my mind.

I get a little pissy with him for not sharing my fantasy. "Hey, when are you going to fix our bathroom sink? Brushing my teeth in the shower is getting old," I grumble. "And that second-floor shutter is going to fall off and kill someone."

Joey gives me a surprised look, followed by a frown. He's not used to me giving him a hard time. I can tell by his body language it bothers him. I feel instantly guilty, but not enough to retract my words or apologize.

"Okay, okay," he mumbles, waving me away like I'm a line cook in one of his restaurant kitchens. But there's a measure of defeat in his tone. "I'll fix the sink this afternoon. Do you know where my tools are?"

Now I'm even pissier and make a face at him. "How would I know where your tools are? Honestly, Joey," Typical Joey. When he doesn't care about something like, say, doing chores or manual labor around the house, he becomes helpless, like a stranger who doesn't have a clue where anything unpleasant, such as tools, could be hidden.

It's not that I'm angry, it's more that I'm frustrated. We ignored making repairs and upgrades to Candyland throughout Jazz's childhood. Joey often worked nights, so when our paths crossed, we only wanted to spend the time together doing fun things. As a chef and museum employee, we lived paycheck to paycheck and didn't have excess cash for home improvements, anyway.

I thought we would focus on Candyland once Jazz was in culinary school. It didn't happen.

I was sure we would finally fix the place once we were retired and had nothing else to do. That didn't happen, either.

I used to have such grand plans for our house—everything from ripping out the sixties Formica countertops, and backsplash and replacing them with granite and ceramic tiles to installing glorious French doors (replacing the rusted sliding door leading to the backyard, the one with the glass that's gone permanently cloudy) if we only had the time, energy, and money.

And, I've been dying to change the color of the walls for years. A fatal miscalculation at the paint store means we have a baby aspirin-colored living room instead of the warm peach I envisioned. Nowadays, I would kill for bright white.

Instead, without even talking about it, things have shifted. A discussion about painting the interior led to a depressing conversation. We would have to empty and move every bookcase and every piece of furniture before we could paint anything, plus the actual painting itself when just our living room alone is two stories. And finally, the topic led to Jazz's plan to sell the house after we die.

An estimate for the price of French doors was so ridiculous that Joey was beyond exasperated. "We're going to pay more for a frigging door than we paid for the house? I don't think so. It's not like we'll be around for forty more years to enjoy it, Linda."

"Don't say that." Joey's words disturb me. Between Marcy's death talk at lunch and now my husband's resignation toward the inevitable, I'm rattled. "What are we supposed to do, just throw in the towel and stop living?

I throw my hands up. "Yeah, we could just be around for only one more day, but with our luck, we'll probably hang in there for twenty more years. Don't you want our house to be beautiful and something we're proud of?"

Joey shrugged.

But I saw his point.

"Who's going to see it and be impressed? Bob and Marcy Garber?" he asked.

No, Joey. That would be me.

But I stayed quiet. Another rare perk of old age is knowing when to pick your fights.

When our refrigerator died last month and we had to go through the excruciating process of researching and getting a new one, Joey turned to me and innocently remarked, "Thank god this is the last one we'll ever have to buy."

"Stop!" I said, mortified. "Please don't go there." It was bad enough Marcy was putting thoughts of death in my head; I didn't need Joey doing it, too.

Chester pressed his little body against me and stared soulfully into my eyes. Tears trickled down my cheeks as I scratched under his chin. *And you're the last puppy we'll ever have.*

One time, while walking Chester, we came upon an elderly man walking an old dog. I could hear him talking tenderly to his dog, matching his pace with the animal's halting, arthritic steps, and I found it almost unbearably poignant. But then the "who dies first and what will be worse" aspect of the moment almost took me to my knees.

I need to shake these thoughts off. Probably because Joey and I are talking about death. I think about Marcy Garber. Time flies. I realize that Marcy and I haven't had lunch together since late spring, when Joey and I were in New York. It's already August.

It's not that I've been avoiding her personally, it's more like I don't want to talk, period.

The whole Jazz and Chaz thing has me down.

I try not to think about it, but it's hard to avoid.

I used to enjoy watching Food Television with Joey. Not that Joey enjoys watching per se, but as a trained chef, he finds their programming, particularly the competition shows, incredibly hokey. His commentary during the shows is hilarious on a Mystery Science Theater level and he appreciates my delighted response.

But now, every time I see Chaz Chipolata, I want to vomit. Just thinking about it now makes me lightheaded.

I can't erase the image of him slinking out of our daughter's bedroom in the middle of the night.

It's just too gross.

Jazz and I have talked a couple of times since New York, but her schedule has been crazy, and it's a FaceTime with Joey standing behind me. I mean, there's nothing more to say.

"Okay, you know what? I'm not going to wait until after lunch. I'm going upstairs to fix the sink now. Wish me luck," Joey quips, breaking me out of my not-so-lovely reverie.

I look up, surprised.

"Hey, thanks, Joey. Good luck!" I mean, I really am shocked. Usually, something like this takes him many months to get to. Oh, who am I kidding? It's never.

"You seem so down lately. I want to make you happy," he remarks. "But I know that I have no idea what I'm doing, so you might have to pull up a YouTube video to help me. Hopefully, I won't flood out and destroy the entire house."

Oh? There's a chance of that?

We have insurance, Joe. Do your worst.

Meanwhile, back on planet Earth, I'm upset that Joey thinks I'm "down." I don't think that is the right word, but what do you call feeling helpless as time passes?

I don't know what's changed with me, but suddenly, I think Joey needs to force a lifetime of living into our remaining years.

How much longer will we be healthy? When was the last time either one of us had a real physical? Now that we're not working anymore, we don't even think about going to the doctor. For all we know, one or both of us is a ticking time bomb.

Candyland is almost a metaphor these days— completely overwhelming, decaying, and bursting at the seams simultaneously. This house needs a Swedish death cleaning. If anything happens to us, Jazz will be left with rooms filled to the brim with forty years of memories.

We have every card she ever made for us, every piece of artwork, every report card. We still have her toys.

Joey has fifty years of rock and roll T-shirts from every concert he ever saw, some so faded and full of holes you can barely recognize what they are.

He refuses to part with any of them.

A horrible thought pushes the boxes of memories to the rear of my mind. What if something happens to Joey? How will I ever be able to go through his things?

I see myself picking up one of his Beatles T-shirts after he's gone. I hold it up to my face and stroke my cheek with it and the image is so powerful, I cover my mouth to keep myself from crying out.

I remember when my parents died and how awful it was to go through their things.

I ended up keeping nothing.

Okay, I need to stop. I'm losing it. Thank god Joey is out of the room.

"Linda! Come upstairs!"

I race up the steps and run into the bathroom. "What?"

Joey flashes a boyish grin, his eyes sparkling with pride. "Look!' he exclaims, turning on the faucet with a flourish. "Ta-da! I fixed it!"

I stare in disbelief, a huge smile lighting up my face. 'Yeah, you did it! Yay, Joey! You da the man!"

"I am," he agrees. "I have no freaking clue what I did, but there's no more leak."

"Ah, the luxury of a working sink." I give him a playful punch on the arm. "I don't know what to wash first."

"Knock yourself out. I'm going downstairs for a snack. Man's work requires man food."

I have no clue what he means by that, but the sink is fixed and all is well in my world. At least for now.

Twelve

Marcy is already at Terroir when I arrive, a half-empty cocktail in her hand. I notice her manicured nails, freshly colored hair, and makeup— a striking transformation.

Sean has my drink in front of me before I'm even sitting down.

"Long time no see," Marcy quips. "My feelings were starting to get hurt."

"*Aw*, don't say that," I reply, waving her off. "Life has been crazy. We're trying to spruce up the house, but mainly, I've been trying to get Joey to help with decluttering. We have forty years of junk crammed into every available space." I make a face. "If I pick something up, there's another fifty things underneath it."

Marcy perks up. "Why? Are you guys going somewhere?"

"Nah, but it occurs to me that if anything happens to one or both of us, we can't leave a mess like that for Jazz to clean up."

Marcy scoffs. "*Pfft*, Jazz will just hire someone with an industrial-sized dumpster. Your place will be empty in a couple of hours."

I stare at Marcy incredulously. Could she really be that cold-hearted? Our entire family's history in a dumpster? But then I remember, she lives in a one-bedroom apartment and she's childless.

Though of course she's right and I agree with her. Possessions are just material things. What does it matter?

Jazz is going to remember cooking breakfast with her dad. She'll recall giggling with me until we were bent over double in Macy's dressing room, trying on ridiculous fancy dresses for a wedding we both know we'll never wear again.

She won't care about her 5th-grade report cards or a vase Joey and I bought on our first vacation together in Ocean City, either.

I think about the boxes of family photos— relics of another time. Who keeps those anymore when everything's on a phone? Who keeps those when everything is on a phone?

Marcy cuts into my thoughts. "So, I have news," she announces.

I stare at her through the liquid in my glass. She's grinning like Cheshire Cat and almost bouncing out of her seat with excitement. So not Marcy. "Oh? Is that why you're going all Swiftie on me? By the way, you look awesome! What's up?"

Marcy grins. "Thanks! Well, you won't believe this, but Bob is totally on board with Belize. Our lease is up December 31 and we'll let the ninety days lapse next month and not renew. Linda, I think it's happening!"

I practically fall out of my chair. This is major, and I'd be lying if I said my first reaction wasn't jealousy, but I quickly recover. Now it's my turn to squeal like a Taylor Swift fan. "What? You're kidding me! Oh my gosh, congratulations! Wait until I tell Joey. Wow, this is amazing. Do you know where you're going to live?"

"Not yet, but I have a couple of contacts there who are sending me leads. You cannot believe what you can get for your money there." Marcy sighs happily and reaches for the menu. "Well, enough about me for now; I'm starving. Do you know what you're going to order?"

"I didn't even check the menu yet, your news is so exciting," I say. Exciting is an understatement. My mind reels from her announcement. I never would have imagined that Marcy, of all people, would live in Belize. But then again, I never thought she'd have an affair with my boss. *Marcy is a mysterious woman.* I shake my head and try to concentrate on the selections. "Hmm, I guess I will have greenhouse gemelli." Something catches my attention on the entrée list.

Oh my god, they have a face bacon burger. Face bacon is a thing?

"Greenhouse whatever sounds too healthy for me," Marcy wrinkles her nose. "Yeah, there are too many vegetables. Am I boring if I have the shrimp again? You have no idea how good it is."

I snort. "Then you should have it. Though you'll probably have fresh seafood all the time where you're heading."

Marcy looks at me glumly. "I wish you two were going with us. But I know, I know," she remarks, holding up her hand to stop me before I start my "where I'd move to" speech. "If you move, it's to Seattle. How's Jazz, by the way?"

I take a swig of my drink, washing down what I really want to say. *Still with Chaz Chipolata, but other than that, doing fine.*

"Jazz is doing great! She's in Tuscany right now to do a series where chefs compete for a chance to train with a master Italian chef. It's a tough life my daughter has."

"Damn," Marcy says.

"I know, right?"

"Ladies. Can I take your order? Sean stands at our table, holding his iPad. "How have you been? Or should I say, where have you been?" He winks at us, a mischievous smile on his face. "Have you been cheating on me with another wine bar?"

"We've been busy," Marcy beams. "I'm planning a move to Belize!"

Sean looks honestly distressed. "Really? Oh no! What about you, Chef Jazz's mom? Are you moving, too?"

"Nah. I will still visit you and I'll bring my husband in for lunch, don't worry," I reply.

"What about Chef Jazz? Does she ever come to Philadelphia?" Sean asks, blushing. He is adorable, with dimples and dark curly hair like my daughter.

"She's in Tuscany now, but always visits for the holidays. I'm guessing you might get to meet her if we're shopping in this vicinity." I assure him.

"I already met her," Sean reminds me.

I don't say anything, but I'm pretty sure there's no way in hell Jazz will remember Sean, no matter how cute he is. Jazz is a star now. She meets hundreds of people every day. When we were in New

York, I noticed she's already adopted the habit of not making eye contact with strangers and holding herself stiffly, not allowing anyone to get too close. And I can tell she's not really listening when they talk to her.

I guess there are trade-offs when you're famous. Maybe that's why she's involved with Chaz Chipolata. They're kindred spirits, these celebrities.

Suddenly, I feel dizzy again. Every damn time I think about those two, I get weirdly lightheaded. I grimace at Marcy, who has eaten every roll in the breadbasket.

I fold my arms across my chest and look at her directly. "Okay, Marcy. Enough about Jazz. Let's hear about you and my boss."

Marcy chortles loudly, and the people at the next table stare at us. Their actions irk me; it'll be a great excuse for Marcy to dodge my question, and I need to know the answer.

Her face flames with embarrassment, and she looks around for Sean. I'm going to need another cocktail!"

I wag my finger at her. "Finish the one you have and spill the beans."

Marcy sighs and slumps in her seat. "Okay. What do you want to know?"

"How did you meet him? How did it start?" I lower my voice, hoping Marcy will do the same. Just in case, I drain my cocktail, so I won't care if she doesn't.

I catch Sean's eye and order another round.

"It was my thirtieth birthday," Marcy mutters. "I came to the museum. You were going to take me to lunch."

Huh? I don't remember that at all. Marcy sees my perplexed expression and smiles.

"It was before there was email or texts. We bumped into each other in the supermarket and chatted. I told you it was my birthday the following day, and we made plans for lunch."

I'm racking my brain, but I have zero recollection of this. *Okay. Think fast, Linda. You and Marcy are the same age. When you were thirty, Jazz was a baby.*

"Jazz was a baby," Marcy confirms, reading my mind. "She was brand new, so tiny you didn't have her even in a baby seat in your shopping cart, you were wearing her in a baby wrap carrier. She was the most beautiful baby I ever saw."

I feel like bawling when she tells me this. "She was," I agree, trying to keep it together.

"You told me you were bone-crushingly tired, working full time, coming home and taking care of her yourself while Joey worked and vice versa for Joey."

I nod my head. "Ah, the sleepless years. No wonder I don't remember. Joey and I were like single parents with our opposite work schedules," I say, trying not to be melancholy.

Marcy smiles sadly. "I was at the worst point of my life. It was my thirtieth birthday, and I was trying to deal with Bob's womanizing and the knowledge we couldn't have kids. I wanted a divorce, but I was terrified of being single. I guess I loved the big goofball. I still love him, don't ask me why," she shrugs.

I lean forward, making sure I hear every word. "So, you and I made plans for a birthday lunch at the museum's restaurant?" I swear, I must have Alzheimer's; I remember none of this.

Marcy stirs her drink thoughtfully. "Maybe I misunderstood you, but that night at the supermarket, you asked me if I had anything special planned for my birthday. I told you Bob was out of town on business, and you said no one should spend their birthday alone, let alone their thirtieth birthday. So I said, 'How about having lunch with me' and you said 'Great!' I took the day off from work and made plans to meet you at your office at the museum."

She stares at me, incredulous that I don't remember this.

I shake my head, trying to clear away the cobwebs. Okay, the first part sounds vaguely familiar, and she probably misunderstood. I probably meant we should have lunch sometime, not a definite date for her birthday, which I clearly must have blown.

But I was so exhausted in those days, anything was possible.

"So, what happened to lunch?" I ask. If she tells me we had this lunch, I'm calling my doctor for a neurological evaluation.

"I went to your office, and you weren't there! They told me you called in sick because your baby had a fever. I remember standing there feeling so let down, it seemed everything bad that happened in the past few months just came crashing down on me, and I burst into tears."

Welp, that explains it.

"Oh, Marcy," I reach across the table and pat her hand because I don't know what else to do. "I'm so sorry."

She smiles and squeezes my hand. "Aw, don't be. It's how I met Claude. He was passing through the suite of offices and saw me crying."

The scene plays out in my head as her words tumble out. *That bastard* is my initial reaction. But too late for my opinion now. "Oh my gosh," I exhale softly, trying to focus.

"I told him it was my birthday, and he took me to lunch. When I finally stopped crying and snapped back to reality, I realized I was sitting across from the most handsome man I had ever seen. He was mesmerizing."

"He was," I agree.

"As we were talking at lunch, we realized we had all these crazy experiences where we just missed meeting each other. We were even both studying painting in Florence the same summer, but at different times." She picks up her drink and takes a sip.

I'm flabbergasted. How do I not know this? I'm an art nerd! I look over at Marcy again. I feel so guilty. I've been a terrible friend. "Wait, excuse me? You studied painting in Florence?"

Marcy seems fine, though. She's smiling.

"Yeah, I went to Florence the summer after I graduated high school. Before I met you, Joey, and Bob in college."

Marcy stirred her drink, lost in the past. "I won a scholarship to study abroad for the summer. I knew my parents were proud of me, but they were having none of my being an artist. They threatened to cut off my tuition if I didn't major in something financially sustainable, so I switched to liberal arts. I thought about teaching, but by then everyone was earning more than teachers, even legal secretaries," she snorts.

"*Gah!* Parents!" I say, as if I'm not one.

"Yeah."

"I paint, too," I tell Marcy. "Or used to. I was going to attend art school, but my high school counselor talked me out of it and steered me toward art history. I think it was her gentle way of telling me if I was planning on living off my modest talent, I'd starve to death."

Marcy laughs. "Yeah. School counselors back then were not exactly helpful. Anything to crush our souls."

Sean brings our lunch, but who can eat? Marcy can, that's who.

She closes her eyes, savoring every bite. "This shrimp," she moans. "I'm gonna miss these suckers when I move to Belize."

She protests when I take her fork away. *Oh no you don't, Marcy, you don't get to change the subject, not before you finish telling me what happened.* "So you had lunch with Claude...Dr. Bissonette...then what?"

"Well, like I said, we had all this crazy stuff in common, and the more we talked, the more exciting it got. It was like we were cosmically meant to meet. It was my thirtieth birthday. I had taken the day off from work, and I was planning on spending the night alone at home getting drunk and crying. Claude and I just kept talking and ordering bottles of wine."

My mouth falls open in shock. "At the museum?"

"Oh, no, no, I left out a part. We only stayed at the museum restaurant for about an hour. When the check came, we were still in the throes of our conversation and neither of us wanted it to end. So, we went to the London Grille down the street. Remember that place? They had the best French onion soup, I'm so sad they closed. Why does everything good have to end, Linda? Can you explain that to me?" Marcy is a little drunk, but then again, so am I.

"I don't know why, Marcy. I wonder that myself."

Marcy sniffs and dabs her napkin clumsily at her nose. "I miss Claude. I miss him so fucking much."

The little candles flickering on our tiny two-top are driving me crazy. Why do I feel so dizzy? I would blow them out, but I can't handle that waxy smell right now.

"So what was the deal with Claude's wife?" I ask, struggling to ground myself. I fan myself with my hand. *Damn, it's hot in here.*

"Lisa?" Macy takes a huge gulp of her drink and sets it on the table, almost missing it. "Lisa had multiple sclerosis. She was diagnosed right after they were married. It was horrible; she was a ballerina."

107

"What happened to Claude in Mexico, Marcy?" I ask quietly.

Marcy's lips quiver. Suddenly, it looks as if all the joy is sucked out of her. For a minute, I almost regret asking. She takes a breath, squares her shoulders, and replies. "He got sick and went looking for a miracle cure. He had ALS. The doctors gave him two to five years at best. Except 'at best' doesn't exist with ALS. Claude bought a gun and took matters into his own hands."

My head is swimming. I've heard enough.

Life is so damn sad.

Thirteen

Jazzy texts me while Joey is at the supermarket. She asks if I want to FaceTime.

"Is a pig's ass pork?" I text back with a smiley face emoji.

I fluff up my hair and put on earrings.

Because FaceTime. I think back to when I was a kid, watching Jetson cartoons. I was horrified by the idea of a telephone with video capabilities and hoped it would never happen in my lifetime. Besides being too neurotic to even go to the Seven-Eleven without clean hair and lipstick, I was someone who lunged for the phone naked and dripping wet right out of the shower. I still can't believe there was never any discussion or protest when it felt like overnight, we all had smartphones with cameras.

"Hi, Mom!" Jazz is outside on her deck. Her curls are gathered in a ponytail and she's wearing aviator sunglasses. She looks more like a supermodel than a chef.

"Hey, Jazz! What's happening? How was Tuscany?" Chester jumps up on my lap and lies down. "Chester, want to say hi to Jazzy?"

Chester looks at me like I'm insane. He might not be wrong.

"Chester! Chester! Your big sister is here," Jazz calls out.

Oh good, she's nuts too. It's all in the family. Yay us.

Chester jumps off my lap and curls up on top of my feet.

"Mom, Tuscany was amazing. You and Dad have to go. You'll lose your mind."

"That's already happened," I laugh. "So what was so great? Besides the food, wine, men, and beautiful scenery, I mean."

"I had dinner in the most fabulous restaurant I have ever eaten at — they shaved fresh truffles on top of our pasta table side and kept going until we said, 'when'. And oh my god, dessert was an Italian chocolate, Charlotte Russe! I'm serious, you and Dad need to do this. I will take you there myself."

"Okay!" Talking to Jazz, I realize I am feeling better than I've felt in days. Jazz is magical. I run my fingers through Chester's fur, and he licks my hand.

"What are you and Dad up to? Still enjoying your retirement, or are you ready to kill each other yet?" Puget Sound glistens behind her. I watch fascinated as a large boat sails by.

I shrug. "Dad and I are good. C'mon, it's Dad," I say.

Jazz smiles. "I love Dad. If only we could get him to move to Seattle, huh, Mom?"

"If only," I sigh.

"So guess what? Chaz thinks we should get married. How funny is that?" Jazz laughs; my heart plummets to my feet and I die a thousand deaths.

I have to shut my eyes for a minute and breathe. "You're not considering it, are you?"

"Mom, are you okay? You look like you're going to throw up or faint." Jazz is clearly concerned,

I can hear the tone in her voice, and I feel instantly guilty for being overly dramatic. But I do feel sick, and it must show.

"Seriously, mom, I'm not going to marry him. I only told you because I thought you would think it's funny."

Oh, it's so hilarious my head is pounding off my neck. "So what did you tell him?"

"I said I'm not ready for that type of commitment." She rolls her eyes and continues. "Mom, honestly, this whole thing is getting boring and old, but that's another story."

Now she really has my attention. Again, my heart pounds. "What do you mean? What's boring and old?"

Jazz turns and stares out at the water for a few seconds and then looks back at me.

"The whole Food Television thing. I feel so out of place; it's not me. I don't want to judge silly competitions between YouTube influencers who think they're trained chefs or use catchphrases like "ooey gooey" and "umami" over and over until I want to puke."

I throw my head back and laugh. Wait until I tell Joey. He noticed the Food Television hosts doing this a while ago and makes a gagging motion every time he hears it.

"It's not funny, it's gross. And, Mom, I don't know if you know this, but rich people…celebrities …are weird. They're not like us."

"Oh, I noticed. Trust me, I noticed. But what do you mean?"

"It's like they're disconnected from reality. Sometimes I feel like I'm speaking with programmed robots without human emotions. There's a whole us versus them mentality, too, and Mom, I'm not an "us", I'm a "them". Does that make sense?"

Woo, does it ever. If only I could jump through my phone and hug her.

"It makes total sense. I worked at a museum; I encountered the *hoi polloi* all the time. I know exactly what you're saying. More than once, I asked myself if these people even had any empathy. I wondered about simple common sense, too."

Jazz's face lights up. "Yes! I knew you'd understand. I love you, Mom."

"I love you, too. So much. I pause, hesitating as her joy reminds me of the complexities in her life. "But I have to ask—if you feel so strongly, how do you rationalize your relationship with Chaz?"

Man, every time I say his name, I can feel the bile rise.

Jazz laughs. "I thought I explained that, Mom."

She laughs harder when she sees my reaction. It's like someone dropped me in a field of fresh manure.

"Mom, Chaz is different. He grew up poor in the Bronx and didn't forget who he is. But yeah, I hear you. It's why I won't let him go public with our relationship. I won't even hang out anywhere with him, which will cause speculation, and I treat him like a stranger when we are in a situation where it might."

She stares out at the water before continuing. My heart crumbles when she looks at me, and there's uncertainty in her eyes. "I know what people will think. I'm not that person. I don't care about fame and fortune. But I like having my own money, so I'm trying to figure out my next move."

My relief at their relationship being private is palpable. Thank god I didn't tell Marcy! Okay, I didn't tell Joey either, but that's because I didn't want him heading to Seattle with a baseball bat. But now Jazz has me upset for other reasons.

"Your next move? Are you thinking of leaving Food Television?" I'm shocked, despite what she's just told me, she seemed so happy there.

"I'm a chef. I love what I do. But I didn't train all these years to stand in a supermarket parking lot judging home cooks competing in a race to see who can use each other's groceries creatively," she sighs.

"Huh? What about a supermarket parking lot?" I ask, confused.

Jazz wrinkles her nose, shaking her head in disgust. "It's a new pilot I just taped, a whole new level of ridiculous. You don't want to know. It's gross."

I frown, her frustration mirroring my growing unease. "*Ugh*, you're right, I don't need any more info; it sounds cheesy." I pause, a hint of hope slipping into my voice. "But can't you convince them to give you a show where you just… cook?"

Hey, I'm her mother, I have to ask this.

Jazz makes a face at me. "Food Television is a shell company for the pork industry," she claims, her voice laced with disgust. "It's all about the advertising revenue. And their marketing surveys say Americans don't like to be educated, they like watching competition shows."

I scowl. "The pork industry, really? I knew it! Food Television is where I first saw chefs putting bacon on everything. Bacon donuts. Bacon ice cream. Yuck!"

Jazz laughs. "You're gonna bring up the banana chocolate chunk bread pudding again, aren't you?"

"You bet your ass I am," I said. "Who would do that to a person? I still haven't recovered.

Years ago, when Jazz was still in culinary school, we went to a new trendy restaurant that Joey wanted to try because the chef had some serious creds.

I told our server I was a vegetarian and that it was my first anniversary of being meat-free. She seemed used to that and recommended a cauliflower dish with harissa, their specialty.

It was delicious, but I was still hungry after I finished. Our server recommended their best seller, the banana chocolate chunk bread pudding.

It sounded good to me.

When she brought it to the table, it looked even better, festooned with mountains of whipped cream and chocolate curls.

I picked up my spoon and sampled it.

"Oh, wow, this is delicious. It has an interesting smoky flavor. You guys gotta try this!"

Joey and Jazz each took a bite, and I saw them exchange alarmed glances.

"What? What's wrong?" I asked them, mystified.

Jazz laughed nervously. "Dad, should I tell her?"

Joey shook his head. "I wouldn't,"

"What? What won't you tell me?" By then I was practically hyperventilating. I didn't know what they were talking about.

"Mom, we think there's bacon in your bread pudding."

And then, well, I'm afraid I became that obnoxious big-mouthed asshole in the restaurant.

"WHO DOES THAT? SOMEONE TELL ME WHO THE HELL PUTS BACON IN DESSERT? I'M A VEGETARIAN AND THEY HAVE TRICKED ME! THEY RUINED MY VEGETARIAN ANNIVERSARY! BACON AND CHOCOLATE? *FEH! FEH! FEH*!"

My freak out was so legendary my family still trots out the story whenever we need a good laugh.

Like now.

"Jazz, all kidding aside, what will you do if you leave Food Television?"

As I wait for her answer, Chester jumps back into my lap, vying for attention. I stroke his fur absentmindedly, my mind still on Jazz's dilemma.

"I dunno. I've been mulling around a couple of things in my brain. Seattle is such a wealthy city. I could be a private chef for an Amazon or Microsoft executive though I would prefer cooking for Eddie Vedder, he lives here, too," she laughs. "But what I've been hot on is pizza."

"Pizza?" I perk up, and so does Chester. He knows the word and what it means. He jumps off my lap and wags his tail. Jazz cracks up.

"I can't believe how Chester fits into this food-obsessed family. That reaction was priceless; you should try to get it on video. But yeah, getting back to what I was saying, the only thing I don't like about Seattle is their pizza. It's total crap. So, in a perfect world, I plan to bring them some East Coast love."

I close my eyes and take a deep breath. I need to find the words that don't make me sound like a helicopter mom. Finally, I ask, "Do you know anything about running a pizza business?"

"Not really," she admits slowly. "But I'm sure I can figure it out. If not, maybe I can bring Dad out of retirement to help me," she says with a smile.

"Yeah, good luck with that," I retort a little huffily.

But on second thought, I can't help but get a little excited. Jazz gets me thinking. Jazz and Joey in the pizza business together? In Seattle? Heart, be still.

I know we're retired. But life is crazy. You never know what can happen.

Fourteen

Now that I have a serious Jazz and Joey pizza shop fantasy going, I declutter Candyland in earnest.

Well, I should say I've been *trying* to declutter. Joey is impossible. He wants to hold on to everything. I take every opportunity to toss stuff out whenever he's not around, like now, when he's walking the dog.

"Where are you going with those newspapers?" Joey's voice booms through the hallway.

Oh no. I thought he was still out with Chester. I feel like a little kid caught stealing a cookie, having to sneak around just to throw things away. But maybe that's my perception. Joey's still oblivious to my pizza parlor dreams and is stubbornly rooted in Candyland.

"I'm just putting them in recycling," I stammer, trying to keep my voice steady. Hidden in those towering stacks of Sunday Philadelphia Bulletin newspapers from thirty years ago, on page 29, is a tiny gem—a photograph of Jazz and her ballet class, posing proudly before their recital. I can't let Joey discover what I'm up to. Not yet anyway.

We've inexplicably held on to five full copies of this newspaper for three decades. There were never any living grandparents to give them to either.

Even more exasperating, there's no mention of Jazz in the article, which merely lists the name of the dance school and the times of the two performances. You can't even tell which fuzzy bear was her. But that's okay...I guess. Our daughter wasn't destined to be the prima ballerina in *The Nutcracker*. After a year of lessons and one recital, she firmly announced she hated ballet and wanted to play softball.

Now I stare at the papers with disgust and hold them at arm's length. "These papers are yellow, curled up, and going into the trash."

Joey stands dejected, as if I broke his favorite immersion blender. He doesn't say anything, but I know it's killing him. I grab the used coffee filter from the coffeemaker and quickly throw grinds over every paper so he can't pull one out.

My plan to Marie Kondo our home, has been more frustrating than I could imagine. In the kitchen, I encounter lids that have no matching pots. How does that even happen?

I don't know why we have any of this stuff.

When we visited Jazz in Seattle last year and I saw her modern, minimalist all white condo, I sighed. Candyland is bursting with objects d'art and flea market finds—everywhere you look, there's something to see. Our shelves are crammed with books and vinyl records. There are antique toys and even a mannequin dressed as a goth.

"You're not going to want any of this, are you?" I asked Jazz during her last visit. My heart plummeted when she made fun of me for having a signed, limited-edition David Bowie action figure in our China cabinet.

Joey and I bought that when we saw David Bowie live at the Tower Theater in Philadelphia when he recorded his infamous live album. It's one of our most treasured possessions from an amazing night.

"Nope," she said, smirking and shaking her head emphatically. "No fucking way. I don't want any of your baby boomer trinkets."

"But it's your inheritance," I said weakly.

All I can say is that even though it pains me to admit this, I understand completely.

I know it's not exactly the same, but I thought my parents were boring and old-fashioned. I felt disconnected from them, which is nothing like our relationship with Jazz. Yet, after they passed away, I threw out all their possessions—everything that represented their lifetime together—with complete certainty.

I should tell Jazz that if I had regrets, that would be my biggest one.

I threw out all physical memories of my mother and father. Sometimes it feels like my childhood was a dream.

And yeah, I know I'm supposed to be a Buddhist and not care about material goods or the past, but that's how it is. I'm not really a Buddhist by any stretch of the imagination, anyway.

I think of what Marcy said the last time we had lunch. "She's just gonna pull up to your house with a dumpster, Linda."

It's weird how history has a habit of repeating itself, huh?

Marcy is the reason I started straightening up today. She's coming over for dinner tonight with Bob. I was doing my usual "company is coming" cleanup. I thought about Marcy and Swedish death cleaning, a euphemism I recently learned that means throwing stuff out so your kids don't have to do it when you die.

I hadn't heard from Marcy for several weeks until she texted me a couple of days ago to invite Bob and herself over for dinner.

What an odd relationship Marcy and I have. Forty years passed without my knowing anything about her. We have a few lunches together. She reveals her skeletons, and now I think about her tangled web of a life all the time.

Her affair with Dr. Bissonette is like a romance novel but with a tragic ending. But I wonder how she could go from sleeping with the world's most exciting, handsome man to "Bob the Nebbish" with his poochy belly and receding hairline.

I shiver when I think of Dr. Bissonette. I wish I had the guts to ask Marcy what he was like as a lover, and then wonder why I care. I need to get a life.

Nah, I might be married, but I'm not dead. I will even fess up to having a long-time old lady celebrity crush on Michael Strahan. I never told my family this because they would never let me live it down. There's just something about him I like, whether it's his athleticism or quick wit, or more like the cute gap between his teeth, whatever, he just does it for me. A couple of years ago, I got stoned and had such a fantasy about Michael that I applied online to be a contestant on *$100,000 Pyramid* so I could meet him.

Oy.

Marcy hinted that she has news. I know when I talked to her last during the summer, she told me they weren't renewing their lease.

But when she disappeared off my radar after our last lunch together, I assumed they changed their minds about Belize.

When Marcy and I had our intimate conversation at Terroir, I would have said one hundred percent that "Marcy and Bob will never move to Belize." But after knowing what I know, I would believe anything.

Marcy and Bob arrive with a bottle of champagne.

Bob hands the bottle to Joey, who turns to me. "Lin, do you know where the ice bucket is? I noticed a few days ago it's not on the counter." He looks back to Marcy and Bob with a huge smile. "What's the occasion, guys?"

I take the bottle of champagne from him. "The ice bucket is on the floor of Jazz's former bedroom. I took it upstairs last week when it rained heavily to catch the leaky roof drippings." I smile and shrug. "No worries, I'll put the champagne in the freezer for a few. It'll be fine. Take a seat in the living room. I'll be right back."

Joey follows me into the kitchen, his brow wrinkling in confusion. "Is it one of their birthdays? Their anniversary?" he whispers.

I plop the bottle in the freezer and shake my head. "No clue. Marcy said they have news."

We walk out together and join Bob and Marcy, who are uncharacteristically sitting next to each other on the sofa.

Bob sniffs the air, his nose twitching with curiosity. "What's for dinner?" he asks, rubbing his hands together in eager anticipation. Marcy, with a playful grin, pretends to slap him. "You're terrible," she giggles.

"Pizza!" I reply brightly.

Bob and Marcy look at each other with such disappointment that I break up laughing. Joey usually makes something a lot less pedestrian.

Joey holds his hands out. "Don't ask me why pizza; I have no idea. Linda's on a pizza kick. She's after me to come up with the perfect crust and toppings. We've had pizza about fifty times in the past month."

I smile innocently.

"Marcy, one pizza has warm shrimp topping like the dish you love at Terroir," I say excitedly. "I told Joey about it, and he recreated it."

"Ooh, that sounds fantastic!" she exclaims, smiling.

I look over at Marcy and do a double-take. It's as if I'm seeing her for the first time. She's lost a lot of weight and looks amazing in her skinny jeans.

Unable to stand the suspense any longer, Joey blurts out, "So why the champagne, guys? What are we celebrating?" He lights up a joint and passes it to Bob.

"We're moving to Belize!" Marcy announces. "Linda didn't tell you?" She looks over at me, surprised. So does Joey.

Joey's eyes bug out in shock. "You knew about this? How did you miss telling me something like that?" he demands.

"You didn't tell me it was definite, Marcy," I protest weakly.

Marcy shifts irritably on the couch. "Sure I did. I told you, Bob and I decided not to renew our lease. I said that when we went out to lunch last month."

"Yeah, but that's all you told me," I argue. "I asked if you found a place in Belize, and you said 'no,' then I didn't hear from you, so I guess I put it out of my mind."

Bob takes a toke off the joint before passing it back to Joey. "We found a place," he announced. "It's practically on the beach!"

Joey stares at all three of us, shocked.

I turn to Marcy, avoiding my husband's gaze. "When are you leaving?"

"Well, our lease runs until December 31. We want to be there for the holidays. We can move in any time after December 15…so, December 15!" Marcy states.

December 15? Much to my surprise, I'm hit with a wave of sadness. "Aw, you won't be here for Christmas," I sigh. All three heads pivot in my direction with the same "since when do you care?" expression.

Bob breaks the awkward silence by whipping out his phone. "Hey, wanna see some pics of our new place?"

"Sure!" I say, glancing over at Joey and trying not to laugh. There are few things Joey hates more than looking at photos on someone's tiny iPhone.

I get up out of my chair and squeeze next to Bob on the sofa. He leans back, scrolling through his phone. "The place is incredible—modern building, right on the water. It's got this huge veranda overlooking a golf course and a pool," he says, showing me a picture of the bright white apartment complex framed by tropical greenery.

"Wait, that's your view?" I ask, leaning in for a closer look. The photo practically oozes relaxation.

"And it's just twelve miles from the Mexican border," Marcy chimes in, her voice buzzing with excitement. "We're talking parks, gardens, and this gorgeous bay to swim in."

Joey, pacing near the kitchen, stops and frowns. "How did you even find this place?"

Marcy shrugs, brushing an invisible speck off the couch. "I told you—those American retirees helped us out. They were amazing. Hooked us up with a realtor who gave us virtual tours."

"Wow, guys, I'm jealous," I blurt. It's the truth.

I mean, I'm not jealous they're moving to Belize, I'm jealous they're doing something exciting and completely changing their lives.

"Get this. It's six hundred dollars a month less than we pay for our crummy apartment now," Bob brags.

Joey still looks stunned. "Have you guys ever been to Belize? How did you find this apartment?" he asks.

"I corresponded with a couple of American couples who retired there," Marcy mentions. "They were incredibly helpful. They put us in touch with a realtor, and we did virtual tours of apartments."

"You guys are crazy," Joey remarks. "I don't think I knew that."

Marcy frowns and shakes her head. "Crazy is staying in Philadelphia," she replies softly.

"Twelve months of sunshine and 24/7 golf, Joe. It ain't crazy," Bob adds.

"Yeah, well…" Joey springs to his feet and begins pacing the room. Change has always unsettled him, and Bob and Marcy seem to embody so much of the past he tries to hold on to. "Who wants pizza?" he blurts out, his voice wavering slightly.

I glance up, briefly concerned, but quickly realize Joey is just trying to calm Chester. The word 'pizza' has sent our dog into overdrive—prancing wildly and nearly hyperventilating at Joey's feet. *Take me with you,* I silently plead, watching as Joey and Chester disappear into the kitchen.

Meanwhile, Bob and Marcy tell me more than I ever needed to know about Belize while Joey makes dinner.

Bob pulls up a tourist brochure on his phone.

"Ambergris Caye is the most popular island. That's where our new apartment is, Linda," he says. "Expats who live on the island enjoy the mesmerizing aquamarine sea while walking the beach, riding a bicycle or a golf cart, which is the primary form of transportation on the island."

"Can you see Bob and me going everywhere together in a golf cart?" Marcy asks, her eyes sparkling. "Nobody has a car on the island, you don't need one. How liberating is that?"

I stare at the kitchen, hoping Joey will come to the door and ask for my help. Anything to get me away from Bob, Marcy, and the talk of their move. The envy boiling in my stomach makes me feel more than a little queasy. I slap on what I hope is a believable smile. "That's fantastic!" My voice sounds high-pitched and unfamiliar.

Bob grins and pulls up another photo on his phone, but I can't bring myself to lean in this time. Instead, I fiddle with the edge of a couch pillow, twisting it as the envy creeps up my throat.

"San Pedro is the island's bustling epicenter. Every Sunday afternoon, local bars and restaurants have barbecues on the beach with live music.

"Now here's something really interesting," Bob mentions, looking at his phone. "Expats living on the island have their pick of an eclectic mix of restaurants, cafés, shops, and even a James Beard-nominated wine bar."

Joey walks in with champagne and four glasses. "Pizzas are in the oven and should be done in about fifteen minutes." He puts a dish towel over the top of the champagne bottle and pops the cork.

We all make the appropriate sounds of appreciation for Joey's prowess. Marcy jabs Bob with her elbow. "Look at that, Joey didn't send the cork flying across the room,"

"Hey, I like the loud explosion it makes when I pop it freestyle! It's festive and goes with celebrating," Bob protests.

Marcy stares at him as if he's a three-year-old caught putting makeup on a cat. "It scares the hell out of me and spills champagne everywhere," she sighs. "It's wasteful."

Joey pours us all a glass and hands them to each of us without commenting.

"To new beginnings," I say, raising my glass and clinking the others.

Joey is silent and looks like he's on the brink of tears. The room feels heavy, despite light-hearted chatter. Bob and Marcy don't notice; they're babbling about golf carts again.

My stomach rocks and rolls. Sweat beads on my upper lip. I grab a coaster and put my champagne glass on the coffee table. I'm so hungry, I'm dizzy.

"Is it fifteen minutes yet?" I mumble to Joey.

"Nope, not yet." Joey leans closer, his brow knitting with worry. His voice softens, but the edge of anxiety is unmistakable. "Hey, are you okay? You're looking really pale. Do you want a hunk of cheese to tide you over?" Joey, Marcy, and Bob all stare, as if I'm going to topple off the couch at any moment.

"I'm fine. I'm just hungry," I say weakly. "I skipped lunch today."

I'm not even a little hungry. I'm nauseous and lightheaded beyond belief.

Can a person make themself physically sick with jealousy? Because that's me right now. I wish I could close my eyes and curl up in the fetal position.

Joey brings out the pizzas.

"I made this one with Linda in mind. It's fresh spinach, filetto tomato, mozzarella, and provolone, baked in a white garlic sauce, topped with grated Romano."

Bob and Marcy *ooh* and *ah*. My stomach lurches. I put my hand over my mouth to keep from vomiting. *Take it away. Please, just take it away.*

Joey continues, unaware my face is probably turning green. "Marcy, this one is dedicated to you. Topped with warm shrimp in a lemon *beurre blanc*. Bob, this baby is for us men. Plum tomatoes caramelized sweet onion, prosciutto, mozzarella, provolone, and Romano. Enjoy!" Joey bows from the waist.

I direct everyone to a stack of plates and napkins on the dining room table. It's all I can manage without risking either hurling or passing out.

Marcy bites into a slice, her eyes widening as she chews. "This pizza is incredible," she exclaims, her words slightly muffled as she takes another bite. "Joey, I'm not even kidding—this is hands down the best pizza I've ever had!"

Joey blushes. "Hey, thanks. I guess it's my new retirement hobby."

"This is fantastic!" Bob exclaims. "What's the meat on this again?"

"Prosciutto," Joey replies. "So glad you're digging it." He notices my empty plate and looks at me, concerned. "Babe, you're not having any pizza? Are you feeling alright?"

"I think I'm having that situation where I was so hungry I made myself sick," I admit. Because really, I feel so awful that I'm afraid if I have even one bite, I'm gonna hurl.

The last time I felt this horrible was last year, when Jazz moved to Seattle. I had to take to my bed for two days and was just about to go to the doctor when whatever it was passed.

I never knew being heartbroken could make you so physically ill.

Marcy, Bob, and Joey scarf down the rest of the pizza and champagne. Joey makes me a cup of tea and watches me worriedly while I curl up in a chair and sip it.

I feel a little better and can feel the color returning to my cheeks. It would suck to be a party pooper on Bob and Marcy's big announcement, so I make an effort to pull myself together.

Marcy smiles fondly at me. "You all good?"

I nod my head "yes".

"I get those spells, too, but I have high blood pressure. You get yours checked lately?"

I raise my right eyebrow and slowly sip my tea, choosing my words carefully. "Yeah, my last physical. I'm fine."

I hope I don't sound as cranky as I feel. One of my pet peeves is people kvetching about their health. Every time Joey and I go to a nice restaurant, we're seated next to elderly couples talking about their last surgical procedures in graphic detail. They all try to one-up each other to compare which was worse. No wonder I don't like going out much anymore.

Marcy gets the hint and changes the subject. Joey always claims I could never be a poker player because my facial expression gives me away every time.

She leans closer, sloshing a few drops of champagne on the floor. "What's new with Jasmine?" Marcy asks. "Whenever I see Chaz Chipolata on television, I think of you guys. I am so jealous. I hope I can meet him someday."

"I'm thinking of inviting him for Christmas dinner," Joey remarks, grinning.

Marcy picks up a throw pillow off the sofa and hits him with it.

Bob squints his eyes and scratches his head. "But…we'll be in Belize. I told you guys that a few minutes ago."

Oy, poor Bob. He's so clueless.

Marcy takes another pillow and playfully bops him on the head. "Joey was teasing me, Bob."

Marcy looks at me, concerned, then pats Bob on his knee. "We should go. Linda didn't eat and looks ready to crash for the night."

Relief washes over me as Marcy and Bob leave. My head pounds, and the lightheaded feeling returns. After promising to meet Marcy for lunch before her trip, and Joey joking about teaching Bob about pizza dough, the door closes behind them with a finality I desperately need.

Joey turns to me and makes a face. "Belize, huh? There's a reason they got a bargain rate for a beachfront property. I worked with a line cook from Belize. He came to America because of the high crime rate there and the inferior medical care…" Joey's voice suddenly trails off and his eyes widen in alarm. "Lin, what's wrong? Are you okay? What's the matter? You're white as a ghost!"

I try grabbing onto the wall to steady myself, but I seem to be slipping. All I can say is, I feel like all the blood is draining out of me, and I have never felt this horrible in my life.

I realize with sudden clarity that I'm dying.

Oh fuck, seriously? This is it?

Before I even get to move to Seattle and watch Jazz and Joey make pizza together?

Before I get to hold any grandkids?

All this time I was worried it would be Joey who would die first and leave me alone and heartbroken.

The joke is on me.

I would weep, but I'm paralyzed. I can literally feel my soul leaving my body.

I struggle to open my mouth and say goodbye to Joey, but nothing comes out.

Life is so goddamn unfair. So goddamn unfair.

And then everything goes dark.

Fifteen

I open my eyes, and I'm in a darkened space with blinking neon green and red lights. Cat Stevens is singing "Peace Train." Every so often, there's a beep that doesn't jibe with the music.

A beautiful African American woman is standing over me, speaking softly. She seems so familiar and comforting, but something is different.

Oh my god, it's my mother.

"Mom? Is that you? You're African American now?"

I knew this is what heaven would look like. Everyone is over-the-top beautiful and there's not a Caucasian in sight.

The Republicans are going to be so pissed. Oh, wait, what am I thinking, they're not going to heaven, they'll never find out. Damn!

My beautiful Nubian mother angel lets out a delighted laugh that sounds like tiny, tinkling bells.

"Oh, honey, I'm not your mama. But it's good to hear you talking. Can you tell me your name?" She's holding a clipboard and a pen.

Heaven has paperwork?

"My name is Linda," I offer weakly.

"Linda, can you tell me your birthday and where you live?"

I answer like a dutiful child. "August 17 and 909 Penny Lane, Philadelphia, Pennsylvania."

I blink a few times, allowing my eyes to adjust. *I'm lying on a gurney?*

A sign over the door reads RADIOLOGY. *Holy fuck, I'm not dead. I'm in a hospital. How did I get here?*

I struggle to sit up and look around frantically. *Joey! Where's Joey? Were we in an accident? Is he okay?*

What happened?

Think, Linda. Think.

I'm consumed with terror.

"Honey, honey, it's okay," the nurse croons. "I'll have the attendant take you to your room now. We just took some blood and a few pictures." She pats my hand reassuringly. "Your husband is already there waiting for you."

Thank god. Joey is okay.

They wheel me into a private room. *Oy vey.* Whatever happened to me resulted in an inpatient stay. When they remove your gallbladder as an outpatient and throw you out an hour after you have *a baby?*

Uh-oh.

Joey stands nervously as the attendant moves me to the bed, his face pale at the sight of the I.V. I muster a weak smile and whisper "Hi," though tears prick my eyes. I feel floaty, less frantic than I should, maybe thanks to the drugs.

"Linda! Oh god, I've been so worried," Joey says, his voice catching.

"What happened? How did I get here? I can't remember anything. Why am I in a hospital?"

"I called 911 screaming like a lunatic. They sent an ambulance and thank god they got to the house immediately. You were out cold."

He takes a breath and continues. "I don't know what happened. You felt a little sick at dinner but then you seemed better. We said goodbye to Bob and Marcy. I started to tell you something, and the next thing I knew, your eyes rolled back in your head and you crashed to the floor…hard. I was terrified you cracked your skull open. What the hell happened?" Joey clutches the bed railing until his knuckles turn white. "Are you sick?"

I shrugged. "I have no clue. Maybe I smoked too much weed?"

"That would be a first," Joey cracks. We laugh, and he looks so relieved. We prefer that explanation to any alternatives.

A nurse walks into the room and takes my vitals. "They're looking over your test results now," she states in a crisp, no-nonsense tone. "The doctor should be in to speak with you shortly." She turns on her heel and leaves before we can ask any more questions, nothing like the angel I met in radiology when I first woke up.

Joey and I look at each other fearfully.

A heavy blanket of dread covers us. Joey furrows his brow and claps my hand. "Linda, listen to me. You fainted because you didn't eat all day and you smoked too much weed," he whispers.

Why is this reminding me of the time Joey tried to blame the upstairs bathroom sink leaking through the kitchen ceiling on the steam from his boiling pasta? Joey can't handle anything bad happening. He can't even acknowledge it.

I'm not so good at it myself. I don't want to alarm him, but I realize I still don't feel well. The floaty situation I'm having might not be from medication I may or may not have been given. Added to that, I have a tight knot of anxiety in my stomach that's making me nauseous.

After (what seems like) several hours (but is probably only fifteen minutes), the doctor arrives with a nurse, pushing what looks like a computer on a wheeled cart.

It *is* a computer.

The doctor introduces himself and, without waiting for us to reply, pulls the computer closer. "Let me show you what you have going on here," he purses his lips and points to the screen.

It's filled with a picture of a human heart.

Joey and I stare at it and then at each other, shocked.

"Okay, I've reviewed your scans and bloodwork; it's pretty cut and dry. The diagnosis is atrial fibrillation. Do you know what that is?" He looks at both of us expectantly and then taps his foot impatiently when we don't immediately respond.

Joey shakes his head. I think I know, but I'm not sure.

My voice rises noticeably, well above its usual level."Did…did I have a heart attack?"

The doctor smiles and shakes his head "no" and pulls the cart with the computer even closer to the bed.

"Atrial fibrillation is when a person has an irregular, often rapid heart rate that causes poor blood flow. Look here," he insists, pointing to the screen. "The heart's upper chambers, called the atria, beat out of coordination with the lower chambers, or ventricles. That's why you fainted." He rubs his chin with his hand, thinking. "Have you been experiencing any symptoms? Maybe lightheaded or short of breath?"

Joey looks at me, concerned. I want to spare him and me, but I must tell the truth.

"Not short of breath, but I have had some dizzy spells. I just thought it was stress because our daughter moved to Seattle and I tend to be a drama queen," I say truthfully.

Joey stares at me with his mouth open. "What causes atrial fibrillation, doctor? And how can it be cured?"

The doctor strokes his chin for a few seconds before he replies. "There are several factors that can cause AFib. Poor quality sleep, smoking, too much alcohol and/or caffeine, excessive exercise or no exercise at all, poor diet, but probably stress is the biggest. Would you say stress is a factor?"

Yes, but I'm not telling you that.

"I probably fall into zero exercise, too much caffeine category," I reply, chuckling slightly. "It's like my body runs on coffee instead of energy. So, what's the magic formula? Cut out the coffee and walk a couple miles every day? Maybe I could even work my way up to a brisk jog--or is that too ambitious for a certified caffeine addict?"

The doctor, however, looks at me like I'm insane.

Hey, if I had my phone, I would have Googled it first and not asked any dumb questions, but no such luck.

The doctor toys with the papers on his clipboard before answering. "There is no cure. AFib is essentially heart failure. I'm going to prescribe several medications that you will take daily, and a blood thinner you'll take twice a day. Right now though, you need a procedure to restore your normal heartbeat. I recommend starting with cardioversion, which is electrical sho"k." He pauses to let the information sink into my and J'ey's shocked minds.

"If that doesn't work, we perform an ablation, which is minimally invasive surgery. You can go straight to ablation and not do the cardioversion but in looking over your chart, I think simple cardioversion should get your heartbeat back to normal."

Cardioversion or ablation what now? I'm fucking stunned and so is Joey.

And heart failure! Isn't that something old people have? Old people who die from it!

"What does cardioversion entail?" Joey asks hoarsely while I mentally compose my will.

The doctor writes something on his clipboard and looks up. "Cardioversion is performed by placing two paddles on the chest. A selected amount of electrical pulses is sent from the paddles through her body to her heart, shocking it into beating regularly."

He smiles reassuringly. "We'll put Linda under anesthesia, and assuming everything goes to plan, she'll most likely be able to go home in a few hours. She'll be able to eat and drink normally afterward and go about her routine. "But," he adds,

137

patting my hand, "if you have any concerns or questions, don't hesitate to ask."

Okay, this sounds good to me, let's not even ask about the other option if this doesn't work.

"I'm good with trying cardio whatever," I reply. Joey nods in agreement.

"Excellent. Okay, we'll get an attendant to take you to our outpatient procedure unit and get you prepped." He turns to Joey with a dismissive wave. "Joe, you have to leave this room now, we have a hospitality suite for family to wait. Any other questions?"

Of course, I want to ask, "Did anybody ever die from cardioversion?" but I stay quiet. I don't want to scare Joey, and honestly, I don't want to know either. If I die, I die. I won't be around to worry about it.

I'm not gonna lie, it's scary as fuck getting wheeled to an operating room. I don't care if it *is* outpatient.

The operating room isn't exactly welcoming. My nerves spike as I'm wheeled in. Where's the anesthesia? I need those drugs—now.

"This will pinch," someone warns. The jab feels more like a stab, but before I can dwell on the pain, darkness washes over me.

When I wake up, I'm in what must be the recovery unit. Bright lights glare down at me, and the noise is almost unbearable. This isn't hell though—at least, I don't see fire or pitchforks.

"Hello, there, sunshine," says a nurse who reminds me of Nurse Ratched in *One Flew Over the*

Cuckoo's Nest. "I'm just going to check your blood pressure. How are you feeling?",

"Pretty good. Can I go home?"

The nurse laughs. I shiver. Her chuckles sound maniacal.

"Soon. I will let the doctor know you're awake, and he'll come in to talk with you and sign your discharge papers."

It's cold in recovery, too cold to be in hell. Groggy, I try to pull the rough woolen blankets higher. "What's the doctor's name?" I ask curiously.

The nurse smiles and pulls the covers up on me. "Dr. Vance," she says with a smile.

Vance? Did she say Vance? Am I sure I didn't die and land in hell?

I think about saying my little joke out loud. However, these days it's hard to predict what people will find funny, so I prefer to stay quiet.

I take a deep breath and slowly exhale. I feel better and man, am I starving.

Dr. Vance appears at the foot of my bed. *Good lord, he even has dark hair and a goatee.* "How are you doing, Linda?

I slap on what I hope is a convincing smile. "I feel great! When can I get sprung? I'm starving and I'd love to grab some dinner. Not that I wouldn't love some yummy hospital food."

"You mean breakfast, it's 7:00 a.m.," he says, smiling back at me. "You can leave as soon as I go over your medication with you. Also, I have you scheduled for a postoperative appointment in my office tomorrow at 11:00 a.m. Everything is in your discharge paperwork. My assistant called your husband to let him know you're awake, and he'll meet you in the lobby when we're finished."

And so, Dr. Vance lays out what my life will be like from now on. I'll depend on five different medications until I die. I learn all about blood thinners and how I can't go anywhere without bandages, because if I even get a simple paper cut, it sounds like I'm going to bleed to death. For that same reason, I can never take aspirin or Advil again. I have to see him, a cardiologist, every six months or more often if I have symptoms or complaints.

I must wear a heart monitor for ten days and keep a journal of how I feel which I enter digitally on an app on my iPhone. My heart monitor is also hooked up to an app.

Yikes. I took my good health for granted. This has me gob smacked. It's like I aged overnight.

"You're going to want to get a daily pill box organizer with sections for morning and evening medication," Dr. Vance says. "Otherwise, it can get confusing, and it's important you don't miss taking your medication daily and on schedule."

Great. I get to have an old lady pillbox now, too.

Please kill me.

On second thought, please don't. You never realize how much you want to live until you have a brush with death.

Yeah, I'll be taking my pills, exercising, and watching what I eat now.

For whatever ridiculous reason, they make me get in a wheelchair, and I must be rolled into the lobby by an attendant to meet Joey. When I see him, I practically leap out of it and into his arms.

We stand there hugging and clinging to each other, oblivious to all the other people and patients milling around us.

"Where's the car parked?" I sniffle.

Joey makes a helpless little boy face. "What car? I came with you in the ambulance. Can you get us an Uber?"

"I don't have my phone with me, Joe. Jesus F. Christ. You need to stop with the Luddite hippie stuff and get a smartphone. How do you not have a phone with apps? How are we going to get home?" I ask peevishly. "What will you do if I die?"

As soon as I say it, I regret it. We're both exhausted. Joey's been up all night at the hospital, worried sick. I've just had my heart electrocuted by two ping-pong paddles.

Joey cringes like I hit him. "Please don't say that," he mumbles.

"I apologize." I'm sincere and feel terrible for yelling at him, especially over something so trivial. "It's been a rough night. Seriously. I'm sorry."

Joey shrugs but doesn't make eye contact. "It's okay. Just don't joke about dying anymore, it's not funny. Can't we hail a regular cab home, or don't they have those anymore?" Joey asks.

"Oh, duh, of course they do," I reply, smacking my forehead in mock realization. "We can get one right on Spruce Street. I'm so used to ordering an Uber that I wasn't even thinking," I admitted, shifting my weight uneasily. I'm still feeling sheepish and guilty for snapping at him earlier, and my voice softens as I look at him apologetically.

A sudden thought occurs to me. I look at Joey, alarmed. "Oh my goodness, what about Chester? He's been by himself all night!"

Joey grins and squeezes my hand. "Chester is fine. I guarantee you he's asleep in our bed right now."

I take a deep breath. I need to stop worrying about everything.

We manage to hail a cab and climb into the back seat. If we hadn't just spent the night at a hospital, we could walk home; it's only about two miles away.

I lay my head on Joey's shoulder and yawn. "I'm still feeling the anesthesia. I'm so tired I could sleep for a week."

My husband kisses the top of my head. "You and me both," he agrees. "But I have to pick Jazz up at the airport in a couple of hours."

I sit up straight. "Jazz? Jazz is coming to Philadelphia?"

"Yeah, I called her while you were having the procedure and afterward to let her know you made it through okay. She insisted on getting a red-eye flight here, anyway."

A lump formed in my throat. *Our daughter is truly spectacular.* "She didn't have to do that," I sniffled. "I'm perfectly fine. The doctor told me I can do everything but drive in the next twenty-four hours, and the "no driving" thing is only because of the possibility of the anesthesia making me sleepy."

In reality, though, I'm having one of those sorry, not sorry moments. Jazz is coming! I try to control my joy.

Joey relaxes against the seat back, but his usual calm is absent. "I was completely freaked out when I first called her. I didn't know what happened and if you would be okay." His voice trembles, and his words trail off as he looks away.

By the time he continues, it's quieter, more measured. "By the time I called her to let her know you came out of the cardioversion, she was already at the airport."

I notice his voice cracking, the weight of the night still heavy on both of us. Reaching out, I touch his arm lightly, offering silent reassurance before leaning in to kiss him.

"Thank you," I whisper.

Joey's gaze meets mine, and I see the unspoken fear lingering in his eyes. "Don't leave me," he murmurs, his words thick with emotion.

"As if," I reply, my tone soft but resolute.

We kiss in the back of the cab like teenagers until my stomach lets out a large, undignified growl. We both laugh because it's such a Linda moment.

"Will you have time to make me a cheese omelet and some home fries before you go to the airport?" I ask Joey, laughing. "I'm a whole new level of starving!"

Oh, crap. Suddenly I remember Dr. Vance standing at my bed, lecturing me about diet, dairy and fried foods.

"Make that some oatmeal," I whimper

Sixteen

Jazz comes bursting through the front door in her usual blaze of fireworks and rainbows while Joey parks the car. I jump up off the sofa to kiss and hug her.

"Mom! How are you feeling? Dad said he made you oatmeal and you couldn't eat it," she says, holding me at arm's length and giving me a closer look.

"I couldn't eat it because unless oatmeal is made with butter, cream, and sugar, it tastes like cardboard," I sulk. "No worries, I ate some peanut butter on toast while Dad went to the airport."

"Natural peanut butter or processed crap with palm oil?" Jazz asks like she's my mother. She's smiling though.

"You know Dad buys all natural," I quip.

He always buys me the honey roasted extra chunky Skippy because he knows I think all-natural peanut butter tastes like cardboard, but I keep that secret to myself. While she's here, I guess I need to hide all my goodies.

Yeah, yeah, I know, "eat to live, don't live to eat," Linda. I read that quote on one of the atrial fibrillation brochures included with my discharge papers.

How can anyone merely eat to live? Good food is everything.

Joey walks through the door, takes off his jacket, and throws it on the sofa. I pick it up and hang it in the closet without comment.

"Dad, we need to hook mom up with a lot of fresh fruit, nut milks, and maple syrup."

"Oh, yummy," I say sarcastically, making a face.

Jazz chuckles, her eyes sparkling with mischief. "Don't worry, Mom, I'll make you a triple berry oatmeal bowl topped with coconut whipped cream. It'll blow your mind," she promises, her voice brimming with enthusiasm. "It's completely vegan, packed with antioxidants, and trust me—you're going to think it's dessert."

I raise an eyebrow skeptically but try to muster some enthusiasm. Jazz's energy is infectious, and I don't want to dim her excitement. Still, the word "vegan" sits uneasily with me. Sure, I can embrace vegetarianism—because, hello, cheese!

My mind drifts to a decadent salted caramel budino with chocolate bark I once savored at Terroir. The memory is so vivid I can almost taste its rich, velvety sweetness on my tongue. So rich, so unforgettable. Sigh.

Ooh, Terroir. A light bulb goes off above my head and I get a great idea.

"Jazz," I begin, a sparkle of excitement lighting up my eyes, "how about tomorrow, after my doctor's appointment, we treat ourselves to one of our classic mother-daughter lunches downtown? There's a fantastic new place I've been dying for you to try. It's close to his office, and we can even enjoy a pleasant walk there."

"Sure, that sounds awesome. What kind of food?"

"Eclectic and very well done," I tell her.

"Hey! What about me?" Joey pretends to be upset.

Jazz laughs. "I'll be here all week, Dad. Maybe we can catch a hockey game together."

The look on Joey's face is priceless. It's like he just won a James Beard award. Hey, he's a chef. No other awards matter.

We're all so tired that we crash for the rest of the afternoon. I hand Jazz clean sheets and towels with an apologetic smile. She's cool with it and makes her childhood bed while Joey and I collapse onto our bed, exhausted beyond belief. I fall into a deep sleep. When I finally open my eyes, I'm alone in the room.

It's dark outside.

I look at the clock; it's only 6:00 p.m. It's almost time to turn the clocks back. For me, it is always the second most depressing day of the year; the day after Christmas being my number one least favorite.

Jazz and Joey are in the kitchen preparing dinner together. I get a lump in my throat, overwhelmed with memories.

Five-year-old Jazz standing on the step stool next to Joey while he showed her how to carefully measure out a cup of flour.

Jazz a few years later, preparing her first Thanksgiving dinner all by herself, with Joey only helping to load the twenty-five-pound turkey into the oven…the always much too huge turkey just for the three of us.

It was always just the three of us every holiday. It's another reason we called each other the three musketeers.

I try not to cry.

Jazz sautés cherry tomatoes and garlic in olive oil. Water boils on the stove for pasta. Joey cuts lettuce for a salad.

I hold up my phone and take probably a hundred photos of them while they laugh and roll their eyes at me.

"Dad, the water's boiling. I'm gonna drop the pasta in. Can you run out to the garden and cut me some fresh basil?"

"Of course, Jazzy," Joey puts down his knife and picks up his shears.

Oh, my heart. My wonky, wonky heart,

Dinner is incredible. I take a few bites and beam at them. I can't stop smiling.

"Look at Mom," Jazz mentions to Joey. "She's so happy.";

Joey smiles broadly at both of us.

He's every bit as happy as I am; maybe more.

"The three amigos," quips Jazz.

"The three musketeers," I reply.

Jazz smiles at me. "That, too."

I'm famished beyond belief and practically inhale my dinner. "This meal was incredible," I say, looking at my empty plate regretfully.

Jazz hands me hers. "Here, Mom, finish mine. I'm not that hungry. I filled up on pizza before you and Dad woke up from your nap."

I look at her, confused. "Pizza? Where did you get pizza?"

Jazz laughs. "Uh, from your refrigerator? I was going to ask you that question. Where did you get that pizza? It might be the best pizza I ever had in my life, and I just came back from Italy!"

Now it's Joey's turn to sit there beaming. Oh my god, she ate Joey's leftovers from our dinner last night with Bob and Marcy Garber.

Why does that feel like a year ago already?

"I made the pizza," Joey tells Jazz. "Your mother is on a 'Joey, try to make the perfect pizza' mission, and you know me, I try to keep her happy," he chuckles.

Jazz looks at me with an eyebrow raised. "Oh?"

"Yeah," I say, looking down and not making eye contact with either of them. What happens next could be crucial to all my secret plans for the future. *Don't blow it, Jazz*, I implore her silently.

"What?" Joey asks, confused.

"Mom didn't tell you?" Jazz is smiling from ear to ear. She's still the little girl who likes teasing me.

Joey stares at me as if he's wondering about how many more secrets I have.

Oy, no wonder I have heart troubles. In the past, I always told Joey everything. I'm not sure why that's changed. I'm going to call it Marcy Garber Syndrome.

"Nobody tells me anything," Joey mopes with such a pathetic expression that we all crack up. "What's the story with the pizza?"

"Well," Jazz continues. "I'm leaving Food Television at the end of this year when my contract's up. I've got my sights set on opening a pizza restaurant in Seattle. You wouldn't believe what they call a thin-crust Neapolitan there. Picture the most awful franchise pizza you've ever had in a shopping mall—but worse. Like Poopy John's."

"You made the decision already, and you quit? Gave them notice? And you didn't tell me that," I say, my voice rising with worry.

She nods yes.

"Are you serious?" Joey looks incredulous. "You're walking away from all that money? What do you know about running a pizza shop?" He turns to me like this harebrained scheme was all my idea. I'm not proud of this, but I entertain the thought of using the atrial fibrillation sickness card and clutching my heart.

"Is this why I've been making pizza five nights a week?" Joey asks, eyebrows raised.

Jazz thinks this is hilarious and bursts out laughing.

"Maybe," I mumble, my face turning red.

"Classic," Joey says to Jazz, and she nods in agreement.

"All kidding aside, Dad, I plan to start with a pop-up event during the holidays. If you can fly out and give me a hand, that would be awesome. And you have some pizza tricks I need to learn."

"We'll see," Joey says gruffly.

I look over at Joey and Jazz with so much hope in my eyes they both start laughing again.

"Laugh away, make fun of me, see if my wonky heart and I care," I say, sticking my tongue out.

I push my chair away from the table and stand. "You guys go into the living room and hang out. I'll load the dishwasher," I pick up a plate and start clearing the table.

"I'll do it." Joey jumps up as if I'm incapable of holding a dish. "Go relax on the sofa. You need to take care of yourself."

I grit my teeth and take deep breaths, willing myself not to lose my patience. "Joey, I'm fine. Please don't treat me like an invalid. It's a minor health issue. If I must be an old lady with an ailment, this is the one to have."

"Dad, Mom's right," Jazz interjected. "I googled it as soon as you told me the diagnosis. AFib can be controlled with medication, diet, and exercise. You can't believe all the famous people who have it," Jazz informs.

"Oh? Like who?" I ask curiously. Hey, I wanna be in the same company as celebrities.

"Miley Cyrus, for one. And Elton John…he's like ninety," Jazz says.

"Elton John is not ninety," Joey snaps.

Elton John was the first concert Joey and I went together as a couple in college and too funny, Jazz was already teasing us about *that* for years but for different reasons.

"Okay, so he's eighty," Jazz laughs. "The main thing is, he's old and living with AFib."

Meh. Meanwhile, I'm not impressed with being compatriots with either Miley or Elton.

"Anyone else?" I ask hopefully.

"Barry Manilow and Gene Simmons from KISS," Jazz snickers. Both she and Joey think this is so hilarious, they dissolve into laughter.

"*Feh!* I want a new disease." I fake scowl and wave them out of the kitchen. "Okay, get out of here and let me clean up. I'll be done in a couple of minutes."

Joey grabs a bottle of wine, two glasses and gives me a look that says "None for you." I don't challenge him. I don't want it, anyway. He doesn't say another word and joins Jazz in the living room.

My mind wanders while I rinse the dishes, and I get the magical idea that everything happens for a reason. I think I once heard it on Oprah, I can't remember, but Oprah or whoever said, "There are no coincidences, it's God whispering in your ear."

I am not sure whether I believe that or not. But…Seattle pizza dreams > atrial fibrillation > Seattle.

When I finish up and join my family, they're halfheartedly watching television. I sit down on the sofa next to Joey and put my head on his shoulder. Jazz and Chester are sharing the dog's chair and Chester is trying unsuccessfully to lick Jazz's wine glass.

I know how you feel, Chester.

I'm pretty sure I can still have wine, but I don't care enough to argue, and I'll ask the doctor about it tomorrow. I'm much more upset about the cheese and full fat ice cream restrictions.

Joey has the remote and is channel surfing. He lands on Food Television. Oy vey. It's the Chaz Chipolata show.

"Hey, it's our buddy, Chaz," Joey says, dropping the remote and raising his glass.

I look at Jazz, but she doesn't meet my glance. Instead, she picks up Chester's tug-o-war and waves it in front of his face. Chester ignores his toy and uses the opportunity to help himself to her wine.

"Chester!" we shout in unison. Chester looks up at us like, "Wut?"

On the screen, Chaz attempts to prepare a rabbit pot pie while a female celebrity judge with a white-blonde mohawk sidles up to him seductively in an effort to distract him.

"Woo, talk about an advertisement for celibacy," Joey chuckles.

My head jerks up.

"More like an ad for birth control," Jazz retorts.

I stare at her wordlessly. There's a lot I could say, but for once I don't.

Mercifully, Joey changes the channel, and we watch a Flyers game. I wish this night would last forever, but it doesn't, and we're all wiped out.

We say goodnight and head to our respective bedrooms. It's like it's twenty years ago all over again; we pick up right where we left off. It just feels so right. I know Joey must be feeling it, too.

The next morning, Joey and I see Dr. Vance together. I get an EKG and the doctor is pleased the cardioversion worked. For now, all I have to do is the medication, diet, and exercise thing, I don't need any further procedures.

The doctor also tells me I'm good to drink wine in moderation; Joey hears it for himself. Smoking weed, not so much.

"I'll do edibles," I whisper to Joey. He puts his arm around me and squeezes me.

Dr. Vance overhears me and jerks his head back. "You are also prohibited from getting a tattoo," he adds, as if the two things are related and I'm some kind of juvenile delinquent.

He doesn't have to tell me the reason for no tattoo is that I'll bleed to death. Unless I'm a complete idiot, that's implied.

"There goes this year's birthday plan," I joke. Dr. Vance doesn't laugh. Neither does Joey.

I text Jazz that I was finishing up and order her an Uber to meet me at Terroir.

Joey drops me off outside the restaurant.

"I'm going to swing by the supermarket on my way home for more pizza supplies," he announces.

I can barely contain my glee.

Seventeen

I'm relieved I get to Terroir before Jazz, and even more relieved when I'm seated and Sean comes to the table.

Sean grins and hands me a menu. "Hey, Linda! How are you?"

I smile back. "Don't ask,"

He doesn't. Damn.

"Is Marcy meeting you this afternoon or are you dining alone?"

"No Marcy today, nope. Someone else, someone you might know," I tease.

"Can I get you something to drink while you're waiting?"

Rats. He still doesn't take the bait.

"Nah, I'll just sip water until my daughter gets here," I say with a little smile.

"Chef Jazz?" he asks, his eyebrows raised.

"Yeah. And here she is." Sean swivels his neck and watches as Jazz bursts through the door in shades of purple and scarlet, her dark curls spilling out of a bright orange wool cap.

Where did I get this child? I'm dressed in the same uniform I wore as a rebellious teenager in 1971: faded jeans and a black t-shirt. Nothing has changed.

Jazz's eyes light up, and she grins from ear to ear. Except…she's not looking at me.

Excitedly, she yells, "Face bacon!" at Sean, before giving him an enormous hug.

Wait, what?

Sean's eyes light up with delight as he laughs. "Jazz! Your mom was just on the verge of spilling the beans about her mystery guest—I'm so glad it's you! It's fantastic to see you again!"

Jazz pats her hair and tucks a lock behind her ear. Much to my surprise, she bats her eyelashes at him. "I can't even believe this," she blushes. "What are the odds?"

"You two know each other?! How? I can't believe it. It's insane!" I stare at both, and a little mind bubble with Oprah inside forms over my head, whispering, "There are no coincidences, Linda."

"Jazz judged my buddy's bar at a burger competition in New York a few months ago. We won with his face bacon burger. Remember I told you I cook nights at a bar in Fishtown? That's the place," Sean explained.

I sit and look at their beaming faces, still not quite understanding what's transpiring. "Wait—the burger competition when Dad and I were in New York? At the food and wine festival?" I ask, shocked. Even after living with Joey for years and knowing how small the food world is, this surprises me.

They say "Yep" together in perfect unison, making us all burst into laughter.

As our mirth fades, Sean smiles and asks warmly. "How about some Prosecco, ladies?"

"Ooh, that sounds good," Jazz comments. "Mom, are you okay with that?"

"Oh hell yes," I reply. "I'm allowed to drink, I just can't get a tattoo."

Sean cocks his head, bewildered, but doesn't say anything. Jazz bursts out laughing.

"Since when do you want a tattoo, Mom?"

I tossed my head and flipped my hair back over my left shoulder. "Since this morning."

Thank goodness she doesn't say anything further about the doctor or my atrial fibrillation. I worry about being that person who over shares medical woes at the table—the kind I avoid sitting near in restaurants.

I can tell Sean wants to linger at our table and chat, but Terroir is a small space, and today it's packed with businesspeople enjoying their lunch break. Normally, Marcy and I avoid the bustle by coming after peak hours, but today Jazz and I find ourselves in the heart of the midday rush.

I can't help myself.I'm in full matchmaker mode. Once a mom, always a mom, I laugh to myself, but still. I'm in love with the idea of Sean and Jazz, the couple.

I need a plan.

Jazz looks at the menu, her brow furrowing in concentration. "So what do you recommend here, Mom? It looks like the chef is far more interested in the vegetarian offerings; the carnivore menu is kind of pedestrian."

She looks up at me, curious. "How's the maitake and trumpet mushrooms with fregola, carrot pesto, sunflower, and preserved lemon? Or do you recommend the Gochujang glazed tofu with miso mash, shiso and Brussel sprout vinaigrette?"

"I've never had either because their menu is seasonal and changes daily," I admit. "But they both sound fantastic. You get one, I'll get the other, and we'll share." I cannot overstate the joy I'm feeling right now. This is our quintessential lunch experience; the same one we've had since Jazz was old enough to sit in a fine dining chair.

She never cried once in a restaurant. Make of that what you will.

Sean comes back with our Prosecco and takes our order. Is it my imagination, or are they smiling at each other nonstop?

Jazz watches as Sean walks away. "That is one good-looking man," she sighs. My mother's intuition high alert antenna pops through the top of my head. I fluff my hair self-consciously. How is it possible she doesn't see them poking out?

I give what I hope is a subtle nod. "He is." Past experience has taught me not to show too much enthusiasm around my daughter—it often leads to suspicion. Especially with men.

I sit back and take a huge gulp of my Prosecco. "So even though I don't want to ask, I have to. What's going on with Chaz Chipolata?"

Jazz laughs. "Still as subtle as ever, huh, Mom? He's in Vietnam. I haven't seen him in a couple of months. I think he'll be home for the holidays. Who knows. Who cares?" she shrugs.

Who cares? I know I don't. Interesting. I wonder why she's so ambivalent.

"What's Chaz doing in Vietnam?" I ask instead. "Don't tell me he's opening up one of his pasta palaces there." I see the billboard in my mind and shudder.

Jazz dramatically shakes her head, feigning deep sadness. "Oh, it's far worse than that."

"Oh my god, what could be worse than a guy with a crown made of gold painted macaroni hawking crappy Americanized Fettuccini Alfredo in Ho Chi Minh City?" I ask with a smile.

"It's way worse," Jazz teases. "Guess."

I have no clue. Unless…

"You're not going to tell me he has a secret Vietnamese wife and kids, are you?" I ask innocently.

Hey, I hope I'm right and he stays there.

Jazz lets out a peal of laughter. "Worse than even that, Mom."

I can't even. My mind is boggled.

"What could be worse? Good lord, he's not doing a reality show there…or a food competition, is he?"

"Haha, you're close!" Jazz leans back in her chair and grins.

"C'mon, Jazz, tell me," I plead. "I can't guess."

My daughter throws her hands up in mock surrender. "Okay, okay. He's doing a series of shows exploring international culture and cuisine. Food Television thinks he has what it takes to be the next Anthony Bourdain." She grimaces, her expression a mix of skepticism and amusement.

"Oh good lord," I groan. "No. Just…no. Please don't tell me he'll comment on the human condition." I picture the Ted Knight character in the *Mary Tyler Moore* show."

"I know, right?" The two of us giggle like teenagers.

Sean arrives with our food. He sets the plates down in front of us. "You two look like you're having a great time."

Jazz and I exchange a smile, then, in perfect harmony, reply, "We are!"

"I love to see it," he remarks. Sean is a genuinely nice person, like Joey. Easygoing and comfortable in his skin. I could never see him wearing a crown made from macaroni unless it was a joke. Or something his young daughter made for him. Holy cow, would Sean and Jazz have a beautiful child!

The thought of a grandchild…I get a knot in my throat and feel like I can't even swallow. I never really knew how much I wanted one. It's hard to believe that until I saw my life flash before me, any fantasies I ever had did not include the thought of Jazz having a baby. Are Joey and I even old enough to be grandparents? Weren't we just in college together, going to a cheesy Elton John concert and sharing a bottle of Boone's Farm Strawberry Hill wine?

Okay, Linda. Get a grip. A minute ago you were laughing uproariously.

Still, I need a plan. I sip on my Prosecco, devising a strategy. *Can I just invite Sean to the house?* Nah, that would be weird. And maybe even desperate, like I was trying to fix Jazz up. I mean, it's true, I am trying to fix her up, but I don't need to advertise it.

"Mom, are you okay? You haven't even touched your lunch," Jazz declares, breaking me out of my reverie.

I give her what I hope is an innocent, nope-not-planning-your-life look. "I'm fine! You know me, I was daydreaming about Dad going to Seattle with you and helping you run a pizza shop. I cut into my mushroom, hoping she bought my fib. "Holy hell, this is delicious."

Jazz crosses her arms and leans forward. "Mom, I'm not opening a shop yet. I thought I would start small, with some pop-up events, and see how it goes. I have friends with restaurants and other businesses in Seattle, including Chaz, who would let me have some space for free or a minimal amount."

I watch enviously as she attacks her tofu with chopsticks effortlessly, like she grew up using them. "My food is incredible, too. And look, Ma, no bacon," she laughs.

"Just face bacon," I say with a grimace.

"Not on your plate, though. I'm surprised you're still being nice to Sean after you just found that he's part of the great bacon conspiracy," she teases.

"He's not!" I exclaim so loudly that Jazz looks up from her food. "I mean," I stammer, "he just helped out his buddy. I'm sure if he had his own restaurant, it wouldn't be on the menu," I say like a little kid.

"You're picking a weird hill to die on." Jazz shrugs. "I get that you like him. You don't have a crush, do you?"

I shivered with revulsion. "Absolutely not! *Ugh*, don't even joke about this—you know me better than that. I love your father. I do admit to being overly sensitive about being fed bacon bread pudding right when I was celebrating my first anniversary of being meat-free," I tell her.

"I wave off her amused expression. "There's a reason I still bring that up all the time. I felt betrayed, and that's a crappy way to feel."

Meanwhile, I'm mortified. This conversation is not working out like I want. I don't care about rehashing the ten-year-old bread pudding story. Instead, I feel like I'm lecturing Jazz for something she doesn't even deserve.

If anything, she's been too honest with me. Though would she have told me about Chaz if I didn't see him leave the apartment at two in the morning?

Probably not; though in her defense, if it is "nothing", why would she tell me anything at all about Chaz? I wouldn't want her to call me and tell me, "Oh hey Mom, nothing is new, but I did meet this rich and famous guy I go to bed with, but no worries, that's all it is."

Yeah, I don't think so. Meanwhile, let's get back to priorities.

"So, these pop-up pizza events you're planning–do you think Dad should come help you?"

Jazz pushes the rest of her food around on her plate. "I would love that. He's going to show me how he does his dough later this afternoon or tonight. He claims the most important part of the process is that the dough must rest for twenty-four hours, which I did not do in all of my pizza experiments."

She pauses and smirks. "Dad says it's the reason his crust is so superior."

I bob my head in agreement. "He really nailed it. His toppings are incredible, too. He makes the sauce by roasting tomatoes from our garden and of course, all the veggies and herbs are also from there so that's another reason Dad's pizza is amazing."

Jazz nods. "Yeah, too bad Dad doesn't have a garden in Seattle. But we have great produce there and amazing seafood. I'm thinking I can make some fabulous pies, especially if I can get Dad's input."

This has to happen.

Sean comes to the table to see if we need anything else; I get a crazy idea.

"Be right back, guys. 'Ladies room." I announce. I quickly stand and immediately start weaving my way through the busy restaurant before Jazz can offer to join me.

Okay, so it's not exactly the most brilliant scheme but it's all I got.

The women's bathroom is private and there's only one toilet. I lock the door and look at the time. Now, how long can I stay in here without anyone thinking I'm pooping or sick? I'm thinking five minutes maximum. If Sean and Jazz are talking, they won't even notice I'm missing. If Sean is busy and Jazz is sitting alone, five minutes will seem excruciatingly long and she'll be so worried she'll come looking for me.

Gah! I feel like I'm in a bad situation comedy.

To kill time, I check social media on my phone. My timeline is filled with ordinary people my age who think we must see a new selfie every day. Especially the men. Yikes. At least I haven't gotten to that point in my retirement yet.

The doorknob turns. Fuck! Someone is trying to get in. But they realize it's locked. Great. Now I have to pretend I went to the bathroom and flush and wash/dry my hands.

I can make that last a couple of minutes but I don't want to be that woman who causes another woman to hop around trying not to pee herself, so I speed it up.

Please don't let it be Jazz on the other side of this door.

I turn the knob and pull. Woo, it's a line of three ladies. Hey, I wasn't in there that long!

Whatever. More importantly, Sean is at our table, engaged in an animated conversation with Jazz. He's still holding the tray with our dirty plates, which means they've been talking the entire time I was in the ladies' room.

Yes!

How does one behave if they don't want to appear too obvious? Don't ask me, I've never been able to perfect it. I take a deep breath and exhale slowly as I walk toward them and slide into my seat with a smile.

But what's this? The come-hither way Jazz is looking up at Sean, her head tilted and eyes shining—and the way he's smiling back at her—can't be my imagination, can it?

I guess it's too soon for me to return to the ladies' room without everyone thinking I have diarrhea. Man, if it weren't for cell phones, I could have pretended I needed to make a call.

"Can I get you two ladies anything else? Dessert? Espresso?" Sean is talking to both of us, but his eyes are only on Jazz.

"Espresso sounds good," Jazz replies, gazing back into his eyes. She reluctantly breaks her stare and turns to me. "Mom, do you want an espresso?"

"Only if I can have it with vanilla gelato," I say truthfully.

"Affogato!" Sean and Jazz say simultaneously and burst into happy shared laughter.

I revert to behavior I've used to make Jazz laugh since she was in kindergarten.

"Huh? Alfogater what now?" They both let out peals of laughter again.

Okay, time for everyone to make fun of clueless Mom and her sheltered, bourgeoisie life.

Like, I don't know that Affogato is a hot espresso poured over vanilla gelato. Like Joey and I didn't go on an Affogato kick for a year. Why do you think I said I wanted it?

Sigh…you'd know that if you still lived in Philadelphia, Jazzy.

They continue to laugh at me, so I cross my arms over my chest and plaster an exaggerated, bewildered expression. Kids today. It's almost painfully easy to fool them.

Eighteen

Jazz and I decide to walk the two miles home from Terroir.

Okay, Jazz decides, there's no way I would have thought of this myself and if I did, I would immediately talk myself out of it. No thank you very much, I will order a taxi.

"Mom, you need to exercise. Remember how we would always walk into town and back together? Now you never go out, and when you do, you take an Uber or a Lyft. You need to think about your health," Jazz points out.

"I have no one to walk with," I say, and regret it instantly. I do not want to play the victim with my daughter and try to make her feel guilty for moving to Seattle.

It wouldn't work, anyway.

Jazz lets out an exasperated groan. "You have Dad. You have Chester. You have ear pods and music. C'mon, Mom. Promise me you'll start walking every day."

"Okay," I chirp. I try not to huff and puff walking up a slight hill, but I feel winded. People walk and talk at the same time? It's been so long, I forgot. Jazz is right. I do need to force myself to go out walking every day.

Ironically, I have issues with Joey for not wanting to leave Candyland and move across the country to Seattle when I am the one having difficulty getting dressed in the morning and walking down the street a few blocks.

I don't know why this strikes me as a revelation right now and what, if anything, I will do with this knowledge. At least it's keeping my mind occupied and I'm not worried about passing out from too much Prosecco and espresso.

But yeah, Joey goes out every day, either to the market or walking Chester. He talks to people. If it wasn't for Marcy Garber, my only non-family conversation in months was with literal strangers—a waiter and a doctor. Now Marcy is moving to Belize. Holy cow, I haven't even digested this yet.

"So, Dad is giving you pizza-making lessons when we get home?" I try to breathe steadily as we walk. So far, so good.

"I know how. I want to see his tricks. Every chef has them." *Mm*, Mom, smell the air. I love autumn. The trees are all lit up in fiery colors. Someone is burning wood in their fireplace, and just the whole anticipation of the holiday season," she says. "I love it."

I bite my tongue to keep myself from asking what her Christmas plans are this year. Does an emergency, unplanned visit to Philadelphia, the first week of November, qualify as an official holiday trip? Oh no, I can't accept that.

But what do I really want? Do I want Jazz to spend money on a return trip in two weeks for Thanksgiving, knowing she'll soon be out of a job?

Here I go, living in the future again. This annoying new habit has to stop. I know it's a minefield for anyone over sixty, let alone someone like me, who spends a lot of time in her head.

Six more blocks to go. I square my shoulders and walk on, determined not to resemble a convalescent grandma. Two minutes later, I begin to pant, and my legs feel like a couple of burning sticks. *Oh my god, this walk is killing me. Note to self: Chester and I will take daily walks together from now on.*

Five more blocks.

"So, how did you enjoy lunch?" I ask Jazz, breaking the silence.

"It was fantastic. If I still lived here, it would be my place." Jazzy's face is healthy, pink, and shining. There's a lilt in her step and tone of voice. There's no huffing and puffing for her. Ah, youth.

"Right? Terroir is the best thing to come out of my forty-year friendship with Marcy Garber. We met for lunch and she picked the restaurant. She hadn't been there before, either. We lucked out," I say. "And we lucked out with Sean, too." I laugh softly and wink at Jazz. "We have our own waiter."

I'm sorry, I couldn't help myself. I had to bring him up. I saw the way they looked at each other. They were flirting!

Jazz doesn't respond. She inhales deeply and smiles.

Four more blocks. Can I call Joey to come pick us up? Or should I call an ambulance?

Oh, I'm fine. I'm just out of shape.

"So, you and Fake Aunt Marcy have retired ladies of leisure lunches now?" Jazz asks with a laugh.

I stop and stare at her, bewildered. "Fake Aunt Marcy? When did you start calling her 'Fake Aunt Marcy'? I don't even remember hearing you call her plain old Aunt Marcy," I say. "I know Dad and I never told you to call her that."

"I've called her Fake Aunt Marcy since I was five when she asked me to call her Aunt Marcy," Jazz replies, her hands gesturing animatedly. "But I never say either name out loud. To me, she's always been Fake Aunt Marcy. Even at five, I knew she wasn't my real aunt. Remember, I asked you?"

"You asked me if Marcy was your real aunt? I don't remember that." It's no excuse; I honestly don't.

Jazz shakes her head and nudges me onward. "Nah, I asked you about aunts, uncles, cousins, and why I didn't have any like all my other friends. You explained it was because you were an only child and so was Dad. And then you said I was, too."

Well, this is an unwelcome trip down memory lane I didn't expect. I do remember. My heart plummets as I recall her reply. "I don't like the words 'only child,' Mommy," Jazz said with a sad little face. It makes me feel like I'm all alone." I remember Joey scooping her up in his arms. We hugged and kissed her and assured we were the three Musketeers and that she would never, ever be alone.

I might die of irony suffocation today. Trust me, it's a thing. People have died from it.

Two more blocks. Maybe I'm going to make it after all. We're finished walking up the hill and are now on flat pavement. I can look down Penny Lane and see Candyland.

"So what's Fake Aunt Marcy up to these days? Besides having lunch with my mama?" Jazz asks.

"Marcy and Bob are moving to Belize next month," I tell her. "Can you believe it?"

"Belize! That's fantastic! What made them do that?"

I shrug. "Oh, that whole second chapter fantasy, I suppose. Belize offers low-cost living on beachfront property for retirees. But Dad tells me there's a lot of crime and less than ideal medical care."

Jazz snorts. "Of course Dad would say that. Belize sounds fantastic. Just don't get any ideas." She puts her arm around me and gives a little squeeze.

No worries.

Whew, we're finally home! I feel like flopping down and kissing the doormat. I walked a couple of miles without having to go to the hospital.

Okay, I seriously need to get a grip. I have AFib, but I'm relatively young and in good health, otherwise. I can't be worrying that I'm going to pass out and die every time I go for a walk.

I just wish everyone my age would stop dying. Damn you, Marcy Garber. Thanks to you, I looked at our college newsletter's "In Memoriam" section. It was shocking to see how many people in our class have passed away. And then I started noticing how many celebrities our age, particularly classic rock musicians, were dropping off like fleas.

Get a grip, Linda. You can't spend the next twenty years worrying about dying, right? Breathe.

Be present. But what if I ignore something serious?
Maybe I need Marcy's therapist's number.

We turn into the driveway. Joey is outside in the garden, planting chrysanthemums as though life were as simple as picking flowers on sale. I exhale, easing back into the present.

Jazz looks up at the house. "Candyland needs some new exterior paint, Dad," she frowns.

Joey scowls back at her. "It's on the list."

Jazz looks at me and rolls her eyes.

I shrug. "Flowers are important, too,"

I'm an enabler, I know, but in my mind, I've already left Candyland. I know its ultimate fate.

"The market was having a sale. I couldn't resist," Joey admits, waving his arms around all the pots.

How can anyone be angry at a man who can't resist chrysanthemums?

A horn beeps, and I jump three feet in the air. Jazz has an expression of surprise on her face, and Joey grins.

"Look who's here," he says.

A bright orange Lamborghini pulls into our driveway.

Ric and Natalia jump out and shout, "Hi!"

Jazz knows who they are right away. She looks at me incredulously, as if to say, "You and Dad have cool friends?"

I hope my return stare says, "We were hip since before you were born."

I begin introductions, but Ric, Natalia, and Jazz recognize each other.

"I'm such a fan of your music," Jazz gushes to Natalia.

"Aw, thank you. I'm a fan of yours, too. Natalia replies. She turns to me, looking contrite. "Linda, I tried texting you before we came by, but you didn't respond. We're in Philadelphia just today; we'd love to get that tour of the house you promised. But if it's inconvenient, we can do it again."

"How do you guys know each other?" Jazz blurts.

Ric raises an eyebrow, a mischievous glint in his eye. "We're old friends," he remarks. Jazz is still a little star-struck, her mouth agape.

"Of course, you guys can come in for a tour," I say, grabbing Natalia by the hand. "Ric's grandfather designed our house," I inform Jazz.

Jazz rolls her eyes. "Seriously? The guy who hung out with the Beatles," she asks. "I've been hearing about that for years."

Ric clears his throat, his cheeks reddening. "Actually…we asked my father, and my grandfather did not go to India with the Beatles to study transcendental meditation. He traveled to India a few years after they did, though who is to say if the Beatles gave him the idea or not," Rick adds, after seeing our disappointed faces.

"My grandfather continued to practice T.M. until he died. I can also tell you that my father and my grandfather were involved in the David Lynch Foundation in Los Angeles, and we all practice T.M., though Natalia and I have our version of daily meditation that helps with our creative process."

Ric cocked his head and looked at us. "I'm curious, though, or should say, my father was curious. Why did you think my grandfather knew the Beatles?"

"Well, it's not just the time frame the house was built, our street is named Penny Lane," Joey explained. "You know, the Beatles' song "Penny Lane"?

Ric erupts into laughter. "Penny Lane was my grandmother. Her maiden name was Penelope Lane."

Now we all laugh because this is all kinds of hilarious.

Jazz and Joey look at me to see how I'm taking the news of no Beatles connection to Candyland, but I'm fine. I'm the one who wants to sell it, remember?

Joey opens the back door, and everyone piles in.

"Oh my gosh, I love your place!" Natalia gushes. "Is this the original kitchen?"

I nod, smiling uncertainly. I usually apologize for our sixty-year-old kitchen.

Natalia is entranced the moment she walks inside Candyland. Her eyes widen as she takes in the cozy charm of the house.

"Oh my gosh, you have a breakfast nook!" she gushes, her voice brimming with excitement. "This is amazing! I've always dreamed of having one. And look at that window seat in the family room— perfect for curling up with a good book! I can't believe it; this place is a dream come true. I don't know why, but I am head over heels for this house. It's just perfect in every way!"

Ric and Joey look at each other. "Women. Who can ever figure out what they're thinking?" Ric quips.

I'm a little mystified by Natalia's reaction to our house. She and Ric have a lot of money. What's the attraction of a run-down split-level over sixty years old?

"I feel something magical here," she says in answer to my unspoken question.

Weird.

We chat for a few more minutes and walk them to their car. They tell us they'll be back in Philadelphia for Christmas and Jazz says she will, too, and we make vague plans to have dinner.

"I can't believe you guys have such cool friends! You should invite them to your Christmas party," Jazz suggests.

Joey pretends not to hear. He gets down on his hands and knees and starts messing with his chrysanthemums.

"We stopped having our Christmas party a few years ago, after you moved out," I tell her, trying to keep my voice even.

"Oh, I didn't realize," she shrugs. "Well, you should have them again. They were fun; I used to love staying up for them when I was a little girl. And then remember when I was in high school, you let me have my friends over? Everyone thought you were so awesome and no one could believe the food. Such good times," she sighs.

I have such a lump in my throat I can hardly talk. Tears blur my vision. I begin working in the yard to keep from bawling.

Jazz gives her father a playful poke in the shoulder. "Dad, are you still up for making some pizza?"

Joey stands up and brushes the dirt off his jeans. "Sure. I'm finished here. Let me go in and wash up. We're just making the dough this afternoon. It has to rest overnight for twenty-four hours. It'll be tomorrow's dinner."

"Yeah, I know, you already told me that," Jazz replies. "I'm going out for dinner tonight, anyway."

Oh? My mom vibes go on full alert. It's like twenty years haven't passed, and I want to hammer her with a million questions about where she's going and who she's going with. But if she hated me for doing it back then, it will be ten times worse now, right?

We all walk back into the house together. Joey goes upstairs to change and clean up.

"You won't be home for supper?" I ask. "Where are you going?"

I'm sorry, I couldn't help myself. The words escape my lips before I can stop myself.

Jazz laughs. "Out with some old Philly friends, where else would I be going? C'mon, Mom, you're giving me a flashback to my high school days. Do I have a curfew tonight, too?"

"You never had a curfew in high school," I say in a huff.

"That's because I was a nerd, Mom," she smiles.

She was not a nerd. Trust me on that.

Joey comes downstairs in a fresh change of clothes.

"Ready?"

"Yeah. Just let me wash my hands. What ingredients are you using, Dad?" Jazz turns on the faucet and grabs the liquid soap while Joey pulls the stand mixer out front and center on the counter.

"Water, sugar, active dry yeast, olive oil, bread flour, and sea salt," Joey answers.

I take a seat at the kitchen table and smile at them.

"She's doing it again, Dad," Jazz groans.

Joey turns around and winks at me. "What's she doing now?"

"Typical mom stuff. Totally over the top, acting all goofy happy." I hang my head down, playing up the role of the dejected and unjustly accused.

Jazz bursts into laughter. "Ha ha, stop Mom, we're ignoring you." She turns to Joey. "Okay, what do you need me to do?" She puts on an apron and looks at Joey.

"Whisk the water with sugar and yeast in the big silver bowl I put on the counter. Got it? Okay. Now mix in the olive oil. Then mix in the flour with your hands or use the dough hook attachment. Your choice," Joey says.

"Dough hook? I don't need no stinkin' dough hook," Jazz laughs, sinking her hands in the bowl. "Then what?"

"After it's all incorporated, cover the bowl with plastic wrap. Then you let it rest for thirty minutes."

"Well, that was easy. Okay, I'm gonna run upstairs and take a quick power nap. See you in a half hour." Jazz kisses us both and leaves the kitchen in a trail of rainbows.

"You realize this is how our life should be every day, right?" I say to Joey, trying not to cry.

"I know," he mutters. "But we're not the ones who moved away. Jazz did."

I'm unsure what he means by that, but it's not the time to ask or get into an argument.

Joey walks behind me and gently squeezes my shoulders. "I'm gonna make some coffee. "Want some?"

I put my head in my hands and rub my temples. "Yes! I have a feeling I'm going to be up late tonight."

Joey looks confused for a minute and then smiles. "Ah, we're waiting up like the old days?"

I look up at him wryly. "Hey, in the old days, we knew all her friends and none of them were old enough to drink. So even more reason to stay awake now."

Joey pours me a cup of coffee, and we sit quietly at the table together. After a while, he takes my hand. "How can you think about leaving this kitchen? So many memories here. So many to come."

"We can take our memories with us wherever we go. If we lived in Seattle, we could have moments like this every day, especially now that Jazz is leaving Food Television," I say, sticking my tongue out at him.

"When did we find enough money to buy a home in Seattle? That's what I want to know," Joey retorts, shaking his head. "The last time you went on this kick, when we visited Jazz, I let you drag me to a real estate office, remember? And what did we find out?"

Gah! I hate it when he gets like this. Especially when he's right. But he's given me an opening and I'm taking it.

"So, hypothetically, if we could afford a house in Seattle, you'd consider moving there?" I ask innocently.

Joey sighs and runs his fingers through his hair. "Sure."

Oh my god, he's such a liar! He thinks he's safe saying that because we looked at run-down, tiny two-bedroom shacks with one bathroom that went for a million dollars.

I read the news; Joey doesn't. Housing prices are falling all over the country.

Jazz comes bouncing into the kitchen. "Okay, I'm back. I totally couldn't nap. I'll take a shower after we're done making dough and maybe I can catch a few Zs then." Jazz checks the time and takes the bowl out of the refrigerator.

So, what's next, Dad?"

Joey shrugs. "Nothing much," he replies with a casual wave of his hand. "It's pretty basic. The real fun will be tomorrow." He looks back over at Jazz and frowns slightly. "Hey, you want to knead the salt into the dough until the dough is totally smooth and all the salt is fully incorporated. Wet your hands, it will make it easier. Now gently fold the dough over onto itself…right, just like that," Joey instructs.

"Okay, got it. Anything else?" Jazz is like Joey, professional and self-assured.

"That's it until this time tomorrow. Cover the bowl with plastic wrap and put it back in the fridge so it can ferment over the next twenty-four hours," Joey tells her.

"So we'll have a pizza party on my last night here. Perfect!" Jazz replies, smiling at us.

My face falls. She's leaving the day after tomorrow? Well, what did I expect? She has a life, and my medical crisis, or should I say "episode," is over.

Live in the present, Linda, I remind myself again. *Don't waste your precious time with your daughter now being sad about two days from now. Talk about unnecessary suffering.*

There's some Buddhism for you.

Jazz shoves the bowl in the fridge and faces us. "Okay, going to shower now and try again for that nap," she says, stretching her arms above her head and letting out a small yawn. "If I'm not awake by 7:00 p.m., please wake me. I'm meeting my friends at 8:00."

"Where are you going?" I ask before I can stop myself. "Do you need a ride?"

"Do you want to take our car?" Joey pipes up.

Jazz chuckles. "Nice to know nothing has changed around here. Mom, I'm meeting my friends downtown, so I'll use Uber. And Dad, there will be wine, so, yeah, Uber." She blows kisses at us as she leaves the kitchen and heads back upstairs. "But thanks guys! I love that you still want to take care of me."

Joey and I just stand around like clueless old people. Man, this feeling is weird. They're not kidding when they say getting older isn't for sissies.

I think about a writer my age on social media—always off hiking mountains or exploring secluded beaches in Normandy.

She seems to wake up every day with the energy of a teenager. Three grown children, miles away, yet her happiness isn't tied to them. If I believe the posts, their bond is strong despite the distance. I admire it, but let's be real: I'm not the mountain-climbing type. Give me wine, cheese, and family, and I'm content."

Nineteen

I hear Jazz get in at 3:00 a.m.

Joey rolls over and mumbles, "Jazz is home" but I'm already at the bedroom window, trying to see who drove her.

"She took an Uber," Joey yawns, reading my mind. "Come back to bed before she hears us. You'll never live down the whole overprotective mother thing if you don't." He pats the space next to him, and I climb in quietly because I know he's right.

I lay awake, wondering who she went out with. Joey and I know all her childhood friends. I would love to know what they're up to now. I don't see why it's a secret. What's the big deal if I ask? I fall asleep thinking if the opportunity comes up, I'm going for it.

The next morning, we drink coffee together, and then Jazz and Joey take Chester for a long walk while I straighten up the house.

I think about Marcy and Bob and how they don't even know I spent a night in the hospital this week.

Dinner with Bob and Marcy feels like a year ago.

Are they too wrapped up in their move to reach out? I almost invite them for Thanksgiving, but what's the point of starting a tradition that won't last? *Gah!* Why am I having daily depressing thoughts? Is this another not-so-tasty side dish of getting older? I blame Marcy Garber.

Jazz and Joey come back from walking Chester.

"Mom, we have news," Jazz exclaims, bursting with excitement. Her eyes sparkle, and her whole face lights up as she can't contain her enthusiasm. "You're going to love this!"

"Well, wait a minute, Jazz," Joey grins. "We need to discuss this with Mom first. She might say no." His voice is steady and warm, helping to ground Jazz's bubbling excitement.

"What? What's going on?" My adrenaline is racing. I look back and forth between Jazz and Joey. They're enjoying messing with me.

"Maybe we better not tell her, Dad," Jazz suggests.

"Tell me what? C'mon, you guys, stop! What news do you need to tell me? Are you trying to give me a heart attack?" I clutch my chest with an exaggerated motion.

Jazz and Joey roll their eyes in unison.

"Mom, remember Shoki, the guy from Seattle who won *Top American Chef* the year I was a finalist? He invited me to do my first pizza pop-up event at his Korean Fried Chicken restaurant on Black Friday! So it's game on! We need to brainstorm a name, and Mom, please don't say Jazzy Pizza, I know that's what you're thinking." Jazz wags her finger at me and laughs. She knows me so well.

"I was going to suggest Pizza by Jazz," I say, sticking my tongue out.

"It should be Pizza by Joey, then," my husband says, shaking his head at us. "Jazz, tell your mother the rest of your news."

I don't like the tone of his voice. More news? Why am I suddenly very nervous?

Please don't let this be about Chaz Chipolata.

And Black Friday? Isn't that the day after Thanksgiving? *Ugh.* So, she won't be here for the holiday.

"Mom, I asked Dad if you guys could fly out to Seattle and be there for support and give me a hand. Dad said he would discuss it with you."

At first, I get insanely excited, but reality quickly sets in. Thanksgiving is in less than two weeks—the absolute worst time to fly. It's crazy expensive and chaotic. And then there's Chester. The last time we boarded him (I swear) he was mad at us for weeks.

But this is the opportunity Jazz has been waiting for. How can I make this work?

"Guys, we can't board Chester on Thanksgiving. That dog will never talk to me again."

I sigh and continue. "Joey, go without me. I'm serious. I'd only get in the way, and this way you can devote all your energy to Pizza by Jazz," I say.

Joey blinks and stares at me for a few seconds to confirm I'm sincere. He's shocked I'm passing up a trip to Seattle, I'm sure.

Jazz smiles and looks at me knowingly, like she sees through my plan.

When you get Dad to Seattle, tell him how much you need his help with your new pizza shop and how much you want us to move to Seattle.

At least that's what I'm hoping for.

Once it's officially established that I am indeed fine with being alone on Thanksgiving, we all agree that Joey should go to Seattle next week so that he and Jazz can prepare for several days before the event. I hop online, look for cheap airline tickets, and learn it's an oxymoron on Thanksgiving. After an afternoon of surfing the web and comparing prices, I finally find something decent, provided he leaves this coming Tuesday, ten days before the holiday and eleven days before showtime.

Other than when Jazz was born and my recent sort of overnight hospital stay, Joey and I have never even spent one night apart. I'm almost giddy at the prospect of being alone for what will amount to two weeks.

"Mom, can you feed yourself for all that time?" Jazz is teasing, but she has a point. I'm far from helpless, but I'm no Joey. The kitchen is his domain.

I shrug. "I'll call GrubHub."

That's an exciting idea. Chester and I can try a new place every night, and I can order stuff Joey won't touch, like vegetarian sushi, cheesecake, or tiramisu for dinner.

Joey *humphs*."You won't need GrubHub, I will cook you two weeks' worth of meals before I leave."

Rats. Foiled again. Well, I'm at least gonna do GrubHub one night.

"Hey, Dad, are we ready to make pizza yet? Jazz interrupts.

Joey looks up at the clock. He runs a hand through his hair, his eyes widening as he takes in the time. "Holy cow, where did today go? Yes, it's time."

We all go into the kitchen. I take my usual seat at the table and Joey takes the bowl of dough out of the refrigerator while Jazz grabs the flour canister.

Joey hands Jazz the bowl. "Okay, Jazz, you want to press your fingers firmly into the dough. Flatten the center—yeah, like that—and work your way out toward the edge until it's about eight inches wide. Pushing down on the dough releases the gas and opens up the dough."

"I know, Dad," Jazz teases, ribbing him a little.

Joey ignores her. "Be careful not to disturb the outermost crust. Okay, now flour your hands, pick it up, and gently stretch it over your fists until it's around fourteen inches."

He smiles and pats her on the back. "You're doing great. Put the dough back on the counter, and dust the pizza peel."

"What's a pizza peel?" I question from the peanut gallery.

Patiently, Joey holds up the thing I call the pizza paddle…the thing you put the pizza on to get it in and out of the oven.

"Oh. I didn't know it was called a peel," I mumble, slipping into the role of clueless mom again. "I call it the pizza paddle."

Jazz and Joey both crack up. Man, they're easy.

"Jazz, now lift and transfer the dough to the peel so you can add the sauce and cheese. And" he added, wagging his finger, "here's a tip. Do not leave the dough with toppings and sauce on the peel for longer than five minutes, or it may stick. Got it?"

"I'm good, Dad. Go into the living room with Mom. I'm gonna make you guys some kickass pizza! Your dinner tonight is gonna rock!" Jazz is in high spirits. Her cheeks are pink and her eyes are shining.

"Our dinner? You're not eating any?" I ask, thinking I'm teasing her.

She shakes her head, still focusing on her work. "Nah, I can't. I'm going out to dinner tonight."

My eyes widen slightly, and I take a deep breath, trying to keep my emotions in check. "You're going out on your last night here? I thought we were having a pizza party!" I blurt out, realizing too late how it might sound. Trying to make my daughter feel guilty is, unfortunately, in my female DNA, and I can't help but let it slip out. Hey, I'm hurt.

Jazz looks surprised. Joey doesn't, I bet he feels the same way I do.

"I'll be home early," Jazz promises. "I'll bring dessert."

She says this as if a piece of chocolate mousse cake will make up for her absence. Well, it will a little, but still…

I'm dying to ask her where she's going; my reason is honorable. I need to look at the menu and pick out what I want. Ideally, she'll bring me home a piece of *lemon* mousse cake.

All kidding aside, I know I better stay quiet and not ask any more questions. But again, I ask myself, who is she going with? Why doesn't she tell me which friends, especially since I know them all and Jazz knows I love gossip?

And then the answer comes to me, and I feel like hurling.

Chaz Chipolata.

He's not in Vietnam, he's in Philadelphia.

I'm gonna vomit.

Instead, I get to eat pizza.

I try to make my mind a blank.

If I don't think about it, it isn't happening.

Jazz's pizzas rock, but if I am honest, Joey's are better. He's mastered the thin, crispy crust. Jazz needs his help. So his trip to Seattle is valid and not some Lucille Ball/Ethel Mertz scheme dreamed up by me.

"Hey, Mom. Do you have a nice dress I can borrow for my dinner tonight?" Jazz asks. She looks at me closely. "We're still the same size, right?"

"I'm a size six still, yes," I say a little indignantly. "But a dress? Me? I gave all my work clothes to Goodwill when I retired. But I don't think I even had one dress to donate." I point to my standard uniform of jeans and a black T-shirt. "When did you ever see me in a dress?"

More importantly, Jazz, why do you need a dress? Though I guess I already know the answer.

"I don't mean a work dress, a cocktail dress, or something fancy. You don't have a little black dress in your closet?" she asks incredulously.

My stomach flip-flops.

"You want a cocktail dress to go out with your friends?" I exclaim, my eyebrows shooting up in surprise. I can't help myself—I'm her mother, after all. But I quickly cover up my blunder. "I have a little black dress, yes, I wore it to functions at the museum. It's got spaghetti straps, though; you'll freeze."

186

Joey looks over at us, finally paying attention. He calls it my sexy dress.

"Let me see it, Mom. Is it hanging in your bedroom closet?"

I gulp and nod "yes".

"Stay where you are. I'll go get it," she instructs. She's already up the stairs before I can even process this and reply.

"This can't be good," I say to Joey.

Joey, meanwhile, is clueless. He's normal and doesn't live inside my crazy head.

"Why isn't it good that she wants to borrow your dress to go out with her friends?" he reasons. "It's bad she wants to look nice? I would think the typical Linda reaction would be '*Ooh* maybe Jazz will meet a Philadelphia boy when she's all dressed up tonight, fall in love, and move back home," Joey says, smiling.

"It's my sexy dress," I hiss.

"She doesn't know I call it that," Joey hissed. His brow furrows, and he lets out a small sigh. "Why are you getting all weird? Are you okay?"

I run my hand through my hair, distracted. "Yeah. Why do you think I'm acting weird?"

"You're not laughing. Normally you would laugh."

"Mom, the dress is awesome. It fits like a glove," Jazz yells from upstairs. "Don't run any water, I'm gonna shower."

I walk to the bottom of the steps.

"What shoes are you going to wear? I might have a pair of size nine heels, I don't remember," I yell back.

"I'm gonna wear my red cowboy boots. It'll look great, Okay, gonna shower. Love you!" she hollers.

"Cowboy boots and a cocktail dress. Only Jazz," I say to Joey. "Of course, she'll pull it off."

She does. When she comes downstairs a half hour later, she looks so drop-dead beautiful that she makes my heart hurt. Her curls tumble down her back, and she's wearing bright red lipstick to match her boots. She's also helped herself to my silver and turquoise jewelry—cuffs and long, dangling earrings.

My stomach lurches. *Eww*, my dress and favorite bracelet are going out with Chaz Chipolata. I can't bear it.

"You look magnificent, sweetheart," Joey says. "Too bad this isn't Hollywood." He beams at her. "Oh, right, you're already a star."

Jazz kisses her dad on the cheek then asks, "Mom, do you still have your blue denim jacket? It's not that cold out yet, and it would rock with this dress.

"Going for the eighties Tina Turner look?" I ask with a smile. "Too bad I don't have any pearls. Anyway, yeah, of course I have a denim jacket. It's in the closet near the front door. Help yourself."

She hugs me, gives me a mischievous wink, and heads toward the door. "Thanks, Mom! Okay, I'm out of here. My ride is a minute away. I'll be home by midnight. My flight is at noon, so I guess you can drive me to the airport around ten. Love you guys! Bye!"

"Midnight?" I say to Joey the minute the door closes behind her. "That's what she calls early?"

"Stop, Linda. She's an adult."

"Midnight is too late for dessert," I reply grumpily.

Joey chuckles, but I feel my mind drifting. Jazz's bold choices—red cowboy boots, turquoise jewelry—linger in my thoughts. It's dazzling, really. Why didn't I ever think of pairing that dress with cowboy boots and turquoise jewelry? Oh, right—I'm in my sixties. The thought stings briefly, but I realize even if I were younger, I wouldn't have worn that look. Maybe this is just the Marcy Garber effect.

Joey and I plop down on the sofa, and Chester jumps up in his chair. He puts his arm around me and stares at me seriously. "You want dessert? I will make you a dessert. What do you want?" Sometimes he's so sensitive, he doesn't realize I'm kidding.

"Lemon mousse cake," I say, crossing my arms over my chest and pouting like a little girl. Now we both laugh.

"I hate that she's leaving tomorrow." I lay my head on Joey's shoulder and sigh.

"I know," he mutters. "Seriously, my plan when I go to Seattle is to lure her back to Philadelphia. Now that she's leaving Food Television, there's no reason for her to be in the same city as their headquarters."

No reason? What do you call a magnificent home on Puget Sound? And a plan to bring great pizza to Seattle.

Meanwhile, the irony of Joey thinking *he's* the one going to talk Jazz into relocating would be hilarious if I didn't feel so strongly about moving to Seattle myself.

We fall asleep in front of the television and wake up around 11:30. Joey makes me go to bed without waiting up for Jazz and I don't even hear her come in.

The next morning, we all load into the car, even Chester, who sits on my lap in the front seat, and drive to the airport.

We pull up to Alaska Airlines, and an angry policeman blows his whistle and motions for us to hurry before Jazz gets out of the car. She jumps out, blowing kisses.

"See you soon, Dad! Can't wait! Love you guys!

And just like that, she's gone in a trail of rainbows, sparklers, and tinkling bells.

Twenty

"You're sure you have everything?" I quiz Joey. "I'm sorry, I can't believe anyone can go away for two weeks with just a carry-on suitcase and a backpack."

Joey looks down and rubs his temples. "I'm not going to Siberia. If I forgot anything, I will buy it at a store."

"How about your boarding pass?" I throw my hands up in frustration. "*Gah*, you and your antique flip phone. I'm just glad we still have a working printer."

"I've got it. It's in the zipper compartment," he assures. "I don't need a smartphone."

"It would have been nice to text you while you're gone," I sigh.

"I'll call." He tilts his head quizzically. "Are you sure you're going to be alright?"

"Of course! I'm gonna be fine."

Woo, am I ever lying. I'm close to tears now.

Now that the time has come, I'm having second thoughts. What was I thinking? I'll be alone for two weeks in this creaky, leaky old house. Not only do I have to feed myself, but I'm also responsible for feeding and walking Chester, even if it's pouring outside. Me, the woman who has spent the last year in her pajamas on the sofa watching television.

I never really think about how dependent I am on Joey. I guess after all these years I take him for granted.

An impatient blast of a car horn jerks me out of my thoughts. I glance out and see headlights in our driveway. *So soon?* I take a deep breath, plaster on a smile, and chatter incessantly; anything to keep from bawling.

"Oh, Joey, your car is here. Holy cow, it's so early in the morning, it's still dark outside. I can't believe this is happening. Kiss me goodbye and call me after you get through security, and don't forget security is on the second floor, you have to take the escalator."

I'm not the only one who appears to be having second thoughts. Joey is white as a ghost. I remember now that he's only flown maybe six times in his life, and it was always with me.

I'm his navigator.

Okay, well, this trip will be good for both of us, then.

We should use this time apart to make ourselves less reliant on each other. It's important. I mean, what happens if one of us…you know.

Joey bends down a little to kiss me goodbye. It's taking me all the willpower in the world not to tell him I changed my mind and don't want him to go.

He stares lovingly into my eyes and then gives me another peck on the lips. "I'll be home before you know it," he whispers.

And just like that, he puts on his coat, backpack, and rolls his suitcase out the door. I stand in the front window with Chester and wave until I can no longer see him.

Can quiet be deafening?

It's 6:00 a.m. The sun isn't even up yet. It's too early for breakfast, and I'm too strung out to go back to bed. Besides, I already had coffee with Joey before he left. I'm so wired I'm jumping out of my skin.

I pick up my phone and check social media. Same old same old. Too many weird unnecessary selfies by men over fifty and graphic descriptions of medical conditions, also with pictures.

Sigh.

No wonder it never appealed to me.

But I guess that's easy for me to say. I have Joey.

I'm not anxious to look up anyone from my past, either. I only dated two other guys seriously before I met Joey, anyway, and I have no desire to see what they look like over forty years later.

It can't be good.

What if I find out they're dead?

I put down my phone and pick up the remote.

I avoid Food Television but it's so early in the morning that nothing else is on but infomercials. I don't feel like committing to anything on Netflix, so I end up putting it on anyway.

Luckily, it's a holiday baking competition. I curl up with Chester on the sofa and watch it the way I would watch a burning building or the aftermath of a car accident. The chefs are supposed to make a Thanksgiving table centerpiece out of cupcakes. Then, just when the bakers are getting ready to put them into the oven, they're given a twist by the celebrity host, an older woman in a bad wig who I swear looks and sounds drunk. They must incorporate an alcoholic beverage into their batter.

This is clearly a rerun from like a hundred years ago. Cupcakes and cocktails are so 2005.

But at least it's pastry chefs doing the judging so I don't have to look at Chaz Chipolata or the other guy who's on Food Television all the time, the one who looks like the second lead singer from Van Halen and visits weird retro bars across America.

I plan to take Chester for a nice long walk as soon as the sun rises. *Oy*. This is only the first hour of day one. Twenty-three more hours and thirteen days to go until Joey comes home.

I consider making myself a full breakfast with eggs, potatoes, and toast; for once, I'm not hungry, and it seems like a lot of work for just one person.

As I half-watch the bakers wrestle cocktail-infused cupcakes, my phone jolts me out of the chaos. Joey's name flashes on the screen, and I immediately answer, relief and excitement flooding my senses.

"Hi!" I practically shout. I sit back and allow his voice to soothe me like a warm, comfortable blanket.

"Hey, sweetie. I'm here. I made it through with no problem. We hit terrible traffic on the expressway getting here, and then the security line was brutal; it snaked around the second floor. It's a good thing you're a nervous wreck and you made me leave as early as I did. So now I'm at my gate and we're getting ready to board. Everything okay?"

"Everything is great," I reply, trying to keep my voice from cracking. "I was just contemplating breakfast and then I'll walk Chester. We miss you already!"

"Aw, I miss you guys, too. Okay, we're boarding! Gotta go! Love you!"

"Love you, too! Safe travels!" I shout into the phone.

The line goes dead.

I feel like crying all over again.

Why did I think it was such a great idea for Joey to go to Seattle without me?

I know I thought of a million things I could do while he's gone...why can't I remember any of them?

Oh, yeah. I've been fantasizing about moving the furniture around in the living room, just to shake things up a bit. I could do that.

But when I start to push Chester's chair, which is heavy, into the middle of the floor, I feel a tug like a muscle pull in my chest.

Uh-oh.

Maybe I shouldn't be doing this when I'm home alone. What if this weird pain is really a heart attack?

Gah! I knew I never should have had lunch with Marcy Garber, now I'm having her thoughts regularly.

Chester jumps up on his now displaced chair and gives me a dirty look as if to say, "See? This is what you get for touching my chair. Now push it back to where it belongs and take me for my damn walk. The sun's out!"

I'm not proud to admit this, but I just said that aloud in what I imagine to be Chester's voice. It came out sounding like Bart Simpson. I amuse myself further by having a conversation with him in his Bart voice and mine until I realize what I'm doing and slap myself back to reality.

"Stand still, Chester. Let me put your leash on." I resist the urge to answer myself.

Chester looks less than thrilled. Joey generally walks him a couple of miles and he's lucky to get a few blocks out of me. Dogs know, man.

"Don't worry, Chester. Mommy will take you for a long walk just like Daddy does."

Chester gives me a woeful look as if to say, "Okay but don't get any bright ideas like you and I wearing matching sweaters. I'm getting nervous you'll be doing tomorrow."

I grab my keys and we head out the door and make a right turn on Penny Lane. During the first block of our walk, I check that I have my keys fifty times because I entertain a horrible fantasy that I lock myself and Chester outside and have to call Joey in Seattle, crying hysterically.

Because there's no such thing as locksmiths. But anything for a vision of impending doom, am I right?

I brandish my fist mentally. *God damn you, Marcy Garber.* I shake it off and force myself to be present.

One of the cool things about Candyland, besides being the only single home in the neighborhood, is the fact that it sits on almost an acre of ground abutting Fairmount Park. As soon as I turn off Penny Lane, I'm at the park's entrance.

This is unheard of in the museum district. We're just blocks from downtown Philadelphia. No wonder we get letters from people who buy houses. I think Joey severely underestimates what our property is worth. The thought occurs that I can find out for sure while he's away by having an official appraisal done, but I quickly discard the idea.

Enough with the secrets.

I enjoy my walk with Chester. It's still peak fall in Philadelphia, and the trees are still lit up in orange, red, and gold. The air is crisp, and someone is frying bacon.

Rather than lament, I am forever cursed by the great bacon conspiracy. I admit it smells good and keep walking. Poor little piggies, though.

Chester keeps turning around and looking at me like he can't believe I'm the one walking him and we're spending a long time at the park.

I'm refreshed and in a much better head when we get home. I feed Chester and make peanut butter toast for myself.

But after I'm done eating, that crushing loneliness sets in again.

There must be something I can do.

Don't I have any hobbies? What's wrong with me?

I put on some classic rock and try to channel my inner creative wild child.

What did I use to do for fun in my spare time? Think, Linda, think.

197

My mind wanders all over the place when suddenly it comes to me. Of course! I'll pull out my easel and art supplies and paint something! Now where did I put everything?

I have to laugh at myself now. The last time I set up my easel and painted, I stood next to Jazz…when she was around seven years old.

I'm thinking that even if I can find my paintbox and brushes, they're all dried up and hard as rocks, unusable. The easel is probably okay, but I think it's in the garage, buried under Joey's mountain of shame, I mean, keepsakes.

Okay, so painting a masterpiece today isn't going to happen but you know what, I can order everything I need online today, and it'll all be here tomorrow.

This cheers me up. I've got Beatles music coming through the speakers and I order everything I could possibly need, from canvas, to brushes, to tubes and tubes of paint in every possible color, and a brand new easel.

This is going to be great.

But once I'm finished ordering, I'm faced with the long, lonely afternoon.

How can it only be 1:00?

Maybe I can take a nap until it's time to eat. At least heating up dinner will be something to do.

Joey left me carefully labeled food containers in the refrigerator and freezer, spanning all nations. There's everything from baked rigatoni to sweet potato black bean burritos. He got so nuts when I said I was going to order GrubHub, he went way above the call of duty when he left me food while he's in Seattle.

Truthfully, I was still going to order Grubhub one night anyway, but now that I just spent a fortune on art supplies, I can't.

It's just as well. Joey's food is better.

I'm not tired. I shut off the music and try the television again. This time I put on Netflix. My problem now is I have too much to watch and I can't decide. Everything looks interesting. I don't want to watch anything too good without Joey.

I finally chose the last couple of seasons of The *Great British Baking Show*. It's soothing, but I won't get super vested in it and won't mind shutting off the television when my paints arrive tomorrow. By the third show, I'm actively rooting for a couple of contestants to get booted.

Damn. This is the longest day of my life.

It gets dark early now. It's barely 4:00 and there's very little light in the room. Outside, the wind is kicking up, and a branch from the tree brushes a window. It scares the hell out of me.

I make sure all the doors are locked and look over at Chester. "You're going out to pee in the backyard tonight, buddy. Tomorrow, I'll take you for a nighttime walk before it gets too dark."

Chester looks at me with his sad beagle face. "I miss my Daddy," it says.

I walk into the kitchen and open the refrigerator. The first container I see is labeled Mushroom Pappardelle. Sounds good to me.

I dump it in a pan and turn on the stove. I don't make myself a salad or heat any bread. When it's hot enough, I spill it into a bowl and eat it standing up by the sink.

Normally, it's one of my favorite pasta dishes Joey makes. Tonight, it could have been cardboard. Without him here, nothing tastes good, nothing feels right.

Sighing, I rinse out my bowl and put it in the dishwasher.

It's 4:30 p.m.

The house feels hollow without Joey. Even Chester looks lost, his beagle eyes searching for his "daddy". I miss my husband more than I should on day one.

Just when I think I am going to lose my mind, the phone rings. "I'm here!" It's Joey. By "here" he means he's at Jazz's place.

"Hi, Mom!" Jazz shouts in the background.

They have me on speaker. I put their call on speaker too, so I can fill the house with sound.

"Hi! So great to hear your voice! Your voices, I mean. How was your flight, Joe?"

"It wasn't bad. You know me, I fell asleep and didn't wake up until we landed," he chuckles.

"*Gah*! I hate you," I say. Joey laughs, and I hear Jazz giggle.

I know it's nuts, but I can't sleep on planes, cars, or any form of transportation. I once took a ten-hour red-eye flight to Germany and still didn't sleep.

There's a reason.

I am convinced that as long as I stay awake, everything will be alright. The plane won't crash. The car won't go off a cliff. The boat won't sink.

Why?

Because I stayed awake.

You're welcome.

I don't care if I'm the butt of every family joke. Make fun of me all you want, but I'm telling you, I keep people alive.

"Is everything okay? What did you and Chester do today?" Joey inquires.

"Everything is fine! We went for a long walk in the park, then we watched television, and later we had dinner," I say, like I'm having a great time doing exciting things.

"Dinner? It's not even 5:00!" Joey laughs and I hear Jazz laugh, too.

"I was hungry," I say like a little kid. "What are you guys doing today?"

"Jazz is going to take me to Ray's for lunch, and then we're going shopping for pizza supplies. We're pretty loose."

"Ray's," I sigh. Ray's is this cool waterfront seafood restaurant right on Puget Sound, a few blocks from Jazz's place. Jazz took us there for dinner the last time Joey and I came for a visit. We ate outside while the sun set on the water, and it was one of the most perfect meals I've ever eaten.

"Aw, we wish you were here, babe. You're sure you're okay?" I can hear the concern in his voice.

"I'm fine. I just can't believe how much I miss you and it's only day one," I admit.

"Same. Anyway, I'm gonna hang up, we just walked in the door from the airport, and it was a long flight. I just wanted you to know I got here fine, and I wanted to make sure everything was good at home. Love you!"

"Love you, too. Love you, too, Jazz!" I say loudly and she hollers, "Love you, Mom" back.

And then silence.

The thought of the long night ahead freaks me out to where I go into the kitchen and open a bottle of wine. I pour myself a glass and bring the full glass and bottle of wine into the living room.

After a couple of sips, I feel better. I roll myself a thick joint and light up. The hell with edibles tonight; one joint won't kill me and Dr. Vance doesn't have to know.

I'm feeling much better.

I pick up my phone and doom scroll through social media again. This time, when I see all the selfies and posts with too much personal information, instead of being annoyed, I feel compassion.

"I'm here, I'm alive, I'm a breathing human being. Please know who I am. Don't forget about me."

Living alone isn't for sissies. Neither is getting older.

I pour another glass of wine and look around the room. There's so many memories. I couldn't bear living here without Joey. Though how could I live anywhere without him?

People manage, I know. No one escapes death and dying.

For the first time, I look up someone from my past on social media. The first boy I ever loved. He turned me on to Quaaludes and the Clash before anyone knew who they were. He was tall and thin with long curly hair. He played the guitar. We dated through high school until senior year when he moved to California with his parents and took my heart with him. There was no internet back then, and when a friend moved even fifty miles away, they were gone forever.

I find him right away because he has an unusual name. And right away, I wish I had never looked.

He's now an investment banker who owns several apartment buildings in Denver, Colorado. He doesn't have long curly hair anymore; he has none, at least that's how it looks; an odd black cap covers his head. He's wearing an austere white button-up shirt and an old-fashioned-looking black suit jacket. He's paunchy.

His wife has her hair covered with a turban. At first, I suspect she has cancer. Looking closer, I realize she's wearing many layers of clothing so that none of her skin is showing. In his profile picture, she stands behind him, looking down.

Oh, jeez, they're Orthodox Jews. I didn't even know he was religious.

Wow. My brain is broken from looking at this photo. All I can think of is popping Quaaludes and hot make-out sessions with insane punk rock music blasting from the speakers of his stereo.

Yeah, I'm not doing this social media stalker stuff anymore.

My college grief counselor was one hundred percent right. Living in the past isn't healthy. It does weird things to your brain.

Okay, now what?

I think about Googling Michael Strahan to see what he's up to and to look at his cute little face and his sexy smile with the gap between his two front teeth. It feels too weird, even for me.

Besides, getting horny certainly isn't going to help matters. Like I'm not anxious enough today.

I put on The *Great British Baking Show* again and sip my wine until finally, this wretched day is over and Chester and I go upstairs to bed.

Today was one of the worst days of my life for no reason at all. I'd been looking forward to the time alone so much and, for whatever reason, I chose to be miserable.

Never again. Tomorrow will be a whole 'nother story.

Thirteen more days to go.

Twenty-One

I wake up the next morning alone in bed. For a moment, I'm confused. Then I remember Joey is in Seattle. I don't like sleeping by myself.

Blech. My next thought is, *Thirteen more days until Joey's home.*

I'm never gonna make it, I'm gonna die of loneliness. Joey's gonna come home to my decomposing corpse.

But then I shake off the doom and gloom. The sun is shining, my art supplies are coming today, and life is good. What the hell is the matter with me? I will not waste today being bored and depressed like yesterday.

Chester and I go downstairs together. He keeps looking at me like, "Where is my daddy?"

I have coffee, Chester has his breakfast, and then we go outside for a glorious stroll in the park.

I have such a great time walking him, breathing in the crisp autumn air, and plotting my first painting. I promise myself that I'm gonna start taking Chester out for a walk at least once a day when Joey's back.

When we get home, I check the tracking information on my art supplies. They're going to be delivered sometime between 11:00 and 1:00.

I decide to make myself a full ridiculous breakfast. Cheese omelet, home fries, and cinnamon toast. I don't remember the last time I cooked for myself.

It turns out this isn't a simple task. I'm not enjoying it at all. I'm having trouble flipping the omelet, and I splash eggs all over the stovetop. *Gah*! I'll have to scrub down the entire stove when I'm done.

Worse, I have the flame too high and the butter in the pan scorches and now my omelet has brown streaks. I fucking hate brown omelets. They taste like dirty feet smell.

I throw it in the trash. But my home fries are gorgeous and calling my name, so I quickly crack two more eggs and scramble them in a fresh pan of melted butter. I'll try an omelet another time.

Okay, breakfast ends up being pretty good. I feel like I accomplished something positive. I take my time cleaning up and enjoy myself doing simple domestic goddess tasks. I can take care of myself after all.

I don't want to think about it, but again I hear this demented voice in my head: *What if something happens to Joey?* I don't want to be one of those sad people who are so dead inside they have to order their pre-packaged meals from Hello Fresh so they can avoid thinking for themselves.

There I go again with the what-ifs. Stop it!

Joey calls to check in and I tell him I made breakfast.

"No! Really? If you didn't take a picture, it didn't happen. Next time you do that, you need to FaceTime me," he teases.

I tell him how excited I am about the art supplies I ordered, and he's happy and supportive.

"Anything that makes you put down your phone," he encourages.

I bite my lip to avoid spewing a heated, maybe hateful, response. I'm not even on my phone that much. I read the news in the morning and use it to shop online. Joey should see what the young girls I worked with were like. They even took their phones with them into the ladies' room stalls when they popped. What a world.

Joey tells me he and Jazz are going to her friend Shoki's restaurant today to check out the space for their pop-up pizza event. After that, they're going to Discovery Park because the November day is sunny and unseasonably mild.

While we're on the phone, there's a knock at the door. My paints are here! I feel almost delirious with excitement.

I tell Joey to have a great day and rush to open my packages. I'm so giddy, I haven't felt this way since I was a teenager walking down the aisles of Philadelphia Art Supply with a twenty-dollar bill.

I have an idea for a painting. An older woman in a darkened room. You can see her in profile with a half empty glass of wine. If I can pull it off, there will be a blurry computer or phone screen in the background casting an eerie light.

I've always been able to draw and paint naturally. I regret never really studying the basics, but maybe that works to my advantage; I'm not bound by any rules.

I lose myself in the painting. Today is the opposite of yesterday. The day flies by and I barely make it in time to walk Chester before dark.

While I'm outside, I get another inspiration, this time for a series of paintings of Candyland. I can do one focusing on our crazy, old-school garden against the backdrop of all the industrial-looking LEGO homes, and another painting of our house being devoured by them. Maybe I will paint a woman in a long white dress with waist-length black hair staring up at the windows longingly.

Today is a success. I'm golden after that.

The two weeks fly by. By my last day home alone, I've completed two paintings and started another.

The paintings I did of Candyland have me fired up. I have so many ideas for future works. The garden in springtime. Little snippets of the interior, maybe the China cabinet with our David Bowie action figure peering out of its glass door.

I'm appreciating this crazy house in a whole new way. Every space represents a new inspiration.

I've also mastered making the perfect cheese omelet. Pale yellow, buttery, and oozing with gooey cheddar and Monterey Jack.

I can't wait to make one for Joey when he comes home tomorrow.

The only time I used GrubHub was on Thanksgiving when I allowed myself to have a pity party. I was fine until I put on the television and watched a few minutes of the Thanksgiving Day parade. I got a flashback of Joey and me taking Jazz to the parade every year.

When Jazz was a little girl, the best part of the parade was that it ended at the Museum of Art, with Santa arriving on its steps. Since I worked at the museum, Jazz had a private audience with Santa every Thanksgiving. It was something special, and it could be why she steadfastly believed he existed until she was in fifth grade.

Joey and I couldn't believe our good luck.

She was so innocent.

So yeah, I got choked up and teary-eyed for a minute there, but then shook it off and pretended I was on holiday instead.

I used to fantasize about taking an exotic island vacation for a week by myself when I worked full time and Joey and I were always crazy busy. I thought going off alone for a week would be amazing and something I'd love.

Welp, I sure know better than that now, huh?

Like most fantasies, they're better off staying in your head and not materializing.

Although Michael Strahan...

So yeah, I pretended I was vacationing on an island in the middle of winter and used Grubhub on Thanksgiving. I ordered a family-sized vegetarian sushi boat, pineapple fried rice, and some fried bananas with vanilla ice cream for dessert.

We shouldn't celebrate stealing America from the Indians, anyway.

The rest of the four-day weekend passes in a happy blur and before I know it, Joey comes walking through the door and it's like the two weeks I spent alone, especially my first trauma-filled day, didn't even happen.

As soon as he's finished saying hello to Chester and changed into his sweats, I ask Joey how it really went.

I had been getting sunny, all positive updates throughout Joey's trip, but always with Jazz in the room. A couple of times I felt Joey was about to tell me something personal, but stopped when she walked in.

"Jazz did great, but I think she realizes being self-employed will not be easy and it's not a good idea to take this on all by herself," he reveals. "If I wasn't there to help, it would have been a shitshow."

"Oy. What do you mean? Wasn't it successful money-wise? Or was it disorganized?"

Joey rolls his eyes. "It wasn't disorganized so much as we had a huge crowd and not enough hands on deck. Plus, it's a fried chicken restaurant with just one pizza oven in the back, and even that was only there courtesy of the former tenant who leased the space. I had to spend a couple of hours cleaning it before I felt comfortable using it," Joey laments, shaking his head.

"And then she was all excited because we made a couple of thousand dollars profit. I reminded her if this was her place, she'd be paying rent, insurance, and regular payroll taxes. I got accused of being a killjoy. So, I don't know what to tell you."

Ugh, the same reasons Joey never wanted a place of his own. I always thought was a shame, but I guess that ship sailed. Or did it?

"Jazz is smart, Joe. She'll figure it out," I assure. But deep down I'm thinking, *She needs us and we need to be there for her.*

I should be thrilled my plan is working, but all I feel is dread. Joey's expression hints there's more to his story. Maybe it's time to grab some wine.

"In other news," he continues tiredly, "Jazz is definitely in a relationship with someone. Every time I tried to talk to her, she was texting with a goofy, lovesick look on her face. I overheard her on the phone a few times too, and I concluded that whoever it was would be arriving for a visit as soon as I left."

My stomach sinks. *Eww. The Pasta King must be back from Vietnam.* I stay silent, forcing myself not to grimace.

Joey raises his eyebrows. "I can't believe you're not asking me anything else. I thought the first thing you would do was yell at me for not questioning Jazz any further. I already had my 'she's a grown-up woman, her love life is personal' defense ready to go. Because it's the truth. I wasn't about to ask her who she's talking to, it's none of my business." He looks at me closely, as if daring me to disagree.

I shrug. "Whatever."

"Whatever? That doesn't sound like you, Linda. Are you angry? Why are you angry?" Joey asks, perplexed.

"I'm not angry. I agree with you. Jazz's love life is her own business," I say.

He erupts into laughter. "Since when?"

I put on my best huffy face. "Since always."

"I call bullshit. Who are you and what have you done with my wife?"

I embrace him, enjoying the feel of my arms around him. Now the world is right. "Joey, right now I'm just happy you're home. I'm exhausted from two weeks of not sleeping very well because I'm used to spooning you and I felt so goddamn alone and cold in our queen-size bed. I even tried to spoon Chester, and he was like, 'Mom, I'm a dog, you're suffocating me."

"Ha! Really?"

"Really."

"Aw, I missed you, too." Joey smiles and kisses my cheek. "Okay, I know you'll find out who the mystery lover is. I have faith," he laughs. "I'm sure you'll tell me as soon as you know."

I know, and I will never tell you. Hopefully, the relationship will end before you ever find out.

The conversation is getting uncomfortable, so I change the subject. "What do you think of my paintings?" I ask shyly.

He looks at each one admiringly. "They're amazing! I think you should do one of Jazzy's place on Puget Sound. Damn, it's beautiful there. The air is different. I dig the vibe."

Oh? Interesting. And yet...I don't feel happy. What the actual fuck. Why?

I'm probably just overtired from not sleeping great without Joey.

"Oh, you know what I wanted to ask you?" Joey remarks. "Can you order me an iPhone?"

"What?" I almost swallow my tongue. "Can you repeat that?"

Joey laughs. "You heard me."

"Excuse me for being shocked. I mean, I've only been begging you to get an iPhone for the last ten years. What brought about this momentous change?"

"I want to text with Jazz," he insists.

"And I can't wait to tell her! I exclaim, excitement bubbling up. "She's never going to believe it."

Joey chuckles. "Oh, she knows. She made me promise that it would be the first thing I did when I got back to Philadelphia."

"Oh, man, let's go to the store now. I'm only half-teasing. We've got to do this before the glow from his trip wears off and he changes his mind.

"I'm beat from my flight, but definitely this week," he promises, surprising me again.

We stand there smiling at each other like little kids.

"So, what else is new?" Joey asks. "Did you have lunch with Marcy while I was gone?"

"Nah, but that reminds me. Bob and Marcy are moving to Belize in two weeks. We need to have them over for a bon voyage dinner, and I should treat Marcy to lunch at Terroir one last time." I sniff like I'm crying, and Joey looks at me, surprised.

"Are you upset they're leaving?" he asks.

"A little," I admit. "Don't ask me why."

Joey smiles. "I don't want them to go, either." He rubs his chin thoughtfully. "Man, this getting older stuff is rough, isn't it?"

"Just a little," I say, rolling my eyes.

I take my phone out of my back pocket and shoot Marcy a text.

She replies immediately, but it takes a minute to absorb what she says.

Huh," I say to Joey. "Well, that's weird." I look down at my phone as if it knows why I'm upset.

"What?"

I shake my head, still not comprehending what I'm reading. "I just texted Marcy Garber and invited her and Bob to the bon voyage dinner party. She said Bob was already in Belize. He flew there ahead of her last week to take care of some paperwork and red tape stuff and to get the apartment set up. Wow! That's it. He's now an official resident of Belize. No more Bob," I mumble.

"You're kidding," Joey says. His shoulders slump like they're carrying an enormous weight, and he looks utterly defeated. "He left without saying goodbye? That's crazy. We've been friends for over forty years."

We shouldn't be surprised. Deep down, I know the truth—we weren't great friends to Bob and Marcy. Not intentionally, but life gets messy. Mistakes linger, and all you can do is try to be better.

"I'm going to have my goodbye lunch with Marcy tomorrow," I tell him. "I'll try to do some damage control, but honestly, I don't think it will be that necessary. I think they're all caught up in their move and didn't deliberately slight us, nor do they feel like we slighted them. I mean, they're getting ready to change their lives. We're probably the last thing on their minds. They're all about turning the page on Chapter One and starting a new and exciting Chapter Two."

Joey nods in agreement. "Yeah, I know they're crazy busy, but I'm not so sure that simply moving to a new location will automatically turn them into happy, interesting people. They might be living on a gorgeous beach, but they're still boring old Bob and Marcy," he points out. "It's not where you live, it's who you are."

Oh?

"No kidding," I whisper.

"Yeah, I realized that in Seattle. When I was sitting on Jazz's deck, watching the sun set on Puget Sound, it was a perfect moment. The only one missing was you," he murmurs, his voice cracking. "Oh, and Chester."

This is the moment I've been waiting for, right?

Right?

Then how come I don't open my mouth and say anything?

Twenty-Two

I'm the first one to arrive at Terroir for lunch today, and that's never happened before with Marcy. I'm just getting ready to text her when she arrives minutes later, all glowy and excited.

"Hi! I was so happy to hear from you before I left! Where's Sean? Did you order us drinks?"

I twist around in my chair. "I haven't seen Sean yet. We need to tease him for being tardy. He usually runs to our table as soon as we walk in."

"I know!" Marcy agrees. "How dare he be late for our last lunch together!"

I sit up straight and stare at her, appalled. "Last lunch? Oh my god, don't say that. It sounds like one of us is dying."

I shake out my napkin and put it in my lap. Marcy does the same. Do people still do this anymore or is it an old lady thing?

"Well, it probably is our last lunch together, Lin. Unless you and Joey can be persuaded to visit us in Belize," she suggests hopefully.

I reach over and pat her hand. "Of course, we'll visit you," I say, my voice filled with heartfelt sincerity.

A slight smile spreads across her face. "Really? You really would?"

Probably not. But my job here is to mend bridges, not blow them up altogether.

"Of course! I'm always up for adventure," I lie.

"Good afternoon, ladies. My name is Emma and I'll be your waitress. May I interest you in a cocktail?"

What's this? No Sean? Our waitress is a beautiful young woman of around twenty, dressed all in black.

"No, thanks, Emma, Sean's our waiter," Marcy blares. "Can you go grab him and tell him Linda and Marcy are here for lunch? Thanks, hon."

Oy. Please kill me now.

Emma pauses, puzzled. "Sean? I'm new here. Let me check." She glides toward the kitchen.

Leaning closer, Marcy whispers, "Sean, right? I'd hate to miss those dimples and that cute little tushy before I leave America."

Moments later, Emma returns with an apologetic tone. "I asked—the chef said Sean isn't with us anymore. He's taken a full-time chef position elsewhere."

"What?" Marcy and I blurt out in unison.

Emma clears her throat and shifts from one foot to the other. "Can I take your order, or do you need a few minutes?"

Marcy gives Emma a peevish look. "We'd like a cocktail first, and we'd like to hear the specials."

I smile, hoping my expression conveys that I'm really a nice person who should not suffer guilt by association.

I channel my last happy visit here with Jazz and suggest to Marcy we order a bottle of Prosecco to celebrate her new life. After all, it's my treat today.

She enthusiastically agrees. Yay! She's going to pass on her usual cheesy "Sex on the Beach" drink. Though, believe it or not, after making her recite all the specials, Marcy orders the shrimp.

She's never tried anything else here.

I think about the conversation I had last night with Joey. You can change locations and say you're starting a new life, but unless you make certain fundamental changes in who you are, nothing is going to change at all.

"So, you said Joey was in Seattle? Just to visit Jazz? How come you didn't go?" Marcy pries.

Emma sets a bucket down on our table, opens the Prosecco, and pours us each a glass before gently placing the bottle in the ice bucket.

"To a happy, healthy life in Belize," I say. We clink glasses and sip our wine.

"Joey went to Seattle to help Jazz with a pizza pop-up event. It sounds like the pizza business is her next new venture. I didn't go because of the expense. Plus, I didn't want to send Chester to the kennel again. He was mad at us for months after the last time."

Marcy nods. "Well, she was smart to enlist Joey. That pizza he made last time we had dinner at your house rocked my world. And you should have called me. I would have watched Chester." Marcy finishes her wine and pours herself another glass. She also tops off mine.

I don't bother responding to her offer to watch Chester. It's moot now, and I'm too tired to engage. I trace the rim of my glass, feeling the weight of everything pressing down on me.

Marcy is leaving, Bob is gone, Sean is gone. My daughter has a secret lover my age (that my brain can't deal with), and my husband suddenly wants what I want, only I don't think I want it anymore.

Gah!

Marcy reaches across the table and pats my hand. "So, nothing else is new? You're so quiet today, Linda. Are you upset about something?"

I pull it away instinctively and then feel guilty. "Aw, no, I didn't sleep very well while Joey was gone," I say. "I think I'm still wiped out."

"Ha! Just the opposite of me. I have been sleeping like a rock since Bob is in Belize. Of course it could be because no one is snoring like a goddamn jackhammer," she laughs. "Meanwhile, I can't believe both our husbands were out of town and we didn't go out one night. We could have gone to a male strip club!"

I stare at Marcy, puzzled. She's kidding, right? I'm not sure. Holy cow, I wouldn't have done that at thirty-five, let alone now. Oy, if women my age are putting dollar bills down the crotches of young, mostly naked guys, I don't even want to know.

"Actually, I couldn't believe how fast the time went. I treated myself to some new art supplies and got involved in painting for the first time in a hundred years," I brag.

Marcy's face brightens. "That's fantastic! Did our conversation at lunch spur you on? I hope so!"

"It might have. Honestly, it was like decades hadn't passed. I picked up the paintbrush like it was yesterday. It just felt so right."

Marcy looks thoughtful, her gaze distant. "I get that. Funny, when I see my new life in Belize, it's through the lens of someone much younger. I fantasize about beach parties and riding a bicycle like a carefree child."

Her wistfulness tugs at something in me, making me smile. "There's nothing wrong with that; it sounds healthy," I agree. "What I meant is, if I can pick up a paintbrush after forty-odd years and have fun, so can you. And you'll have that gorgeous new setting as a backdrop for inspiration."

I laugh softly. "You should have seen me last week, rediscovering nooks and crannies all over Candyland and using them as ideas. I already have two paintings finished as part of a series I'm doing," I tell her. "You should swing by for dinner before you leave and give me a critique."

I sit back in my chair and smile, feeling very pleased. Damage control is officially complete, and I get to show off my artwork to Marcy.

Marcy sighs and shakes her head sadly. "Aw, I wish I could, but I'm outta here in just two days and I'm not finished packing. Can you believe it? Tomorrow is the big day as far as taking out the trash. I'm going to need my energy."

Her words hit me like a freight train, derailing my thoughts. "Taking out the trash?" I echo, my confusion blending with disbelief. My brain struggles to accept that she's leaving so soon—I could have sworn she had a couple more weeks.

"Well, yeah. Bob and I lived in that apartment for decades and there's nothing I want to take with me. I'm like a bride, I want everything new from dishes to sheets," Marcy cheerfully exclaims.

I stare at her and try to absorb her comment. I get what she's saying but it's making my stomach hurt. She's just going to throw out her entire former life?

Wait until I tell Joey.

When I think about moving to Seattle, I think about moving all our possessions with us. Not five copies of a newspaper or a couple hundred t-shirts, but our beautiful furniture, our art, our books, our vinyl, our dishes, and all the crazy knickknacks…our possessions that fill our twenty-five hundred square foot home.

Was I planning on driving it all in a tractor-trailer three thousand miles across America and stuffing it into a nine-hundred-square-foot condo in Seattle? Or throwing it all out like Bob and Marcy Garber?

Yeah, we're not moving any time soon. What was I thinking?

Marcy and I finish lunch in an awkward conversation. I keep asking her questions about Belize, but my mind wanders when she replies. I'm barely listening, struggling to keep my eyes focused on her and at least pretend to be engaged.

"So what time is your flight?" I inquire.

She stares at me strangely. "I just told you. I leave at 7:00 a.m."

Her response sends a pang through me, sharp and unfamiliar. "I'm sorry, Marcy. I'm not handling this well. Change is rough on us old people." I don't know why, but my eyes fill up with tears.

Marcy smiles. "I understand. We have a history. We grew up together," she mumbles.

Oh, great. Here comes the waterworks.

"I am going to visit you for sure," I sniff.

"You better," she whimpers.

Emma asks if we want dessert, but neither of us is in the mood. I ask her for the check, and she hands it to me before discreetly slipping away. I figure out the tip, sign the receipt, take my card out of my wallet, and insert it into the check's billfold. Done and done.

"Hey, I forgot to tell you, Joey is getting an iPhone," I say.

"You're kidding me! It's the end of an era," Marcy says with a huge smile.

"Right? It's like everything is changing all at once," I reply. "First Jazz moves to Seattle. Then you and Bob retire to Belize. No more Sean at Terroir, and now Joey wants an iPhone. What's next? Candyland gets historically certified?" I am trying to keep my voice light, but I am seriously getting ready to cry.

What I don't add is that overnight I went from being a healthy woman to a heart patient who takes eighty-seven different pills every day. And then there's the tattoo—I never wanted one, but somehow, losing that choice stings. The smallest freedoms seem precious once they're gone.

"Hey, it could happen," Marcy smiles. "It certainly is unique."

"What?" Marcy snaps me out of my dark thoughts, but I have no idea what she's talking about.

"Candyland could get historically certified," she smiles.

"Haha yeah, as what, though?" I smile back.

Emma returns with my card and thanks us.

The big goodbye I pictured with Sean didn't happen. I don't know why I'm so upset that I'll never see him again. Have I become so isolated from society that I automatically feel close to anyone who is kind to me and makes me feel happy?

Marcy and I put on our coats and exit the restaurant. We stand outside, squinting in the late afternoon sunlight.

"It's a lot of fun trying to order an Uber on your phone when you can hardly see, isn't it?" Marcy says, waving her phone at me.

"Yeah, this is a real cabaret," I reply, squinting and waving my phone back at her. "I probably need cataract surgery on top of everything else." I sigh, but I manage to order my ride.

"Welcome to our golden years," Marcy snorts.

I snort along with her, despite myself. "Golden, huh? More like tin," I say. "The tin years."

"Tin when it gets all green and moldy looking," Marcy says, shaking her head.

"This is some send-off I'm giving you," I remark sadly. "I'm sorry."

"I had a blast," Marcy says. "Thanks for lunch today, and thanks for everything." She pauses and takes a deep breath. "I mean it. You and Joey are an inspiration." She wipes her eyes and gives me a watery smile. "Now get your act together and move your ass to Seattle, okay? Love you!"

"Aw, okay. Love you, too, Marcy. Safe travels…and…and have a nice life. You and Bob deserve it." My voice wavers, and the words stick in my throat. As I watch her Uber pull away, the finality hits me harder than I expected. Another piece of my world is shifting, slipping away, and I'm left clinging to the edges.

Twenty-Three

Joey gets his new iPhone and, much to my shock, spends serious time trying to learn how to use it. He gets easily frustrated.

"How do I add phone numbers?" he demands.

I give him a quick lesson, giggling as I watch him clumsily try to add me to his contacts. He is not amused and gives me a dirty look, which I ignore.

"Okay, can you put in Jazz's number?" he asks, sounding like a little boy.

I pretend to be annoyed. "Joey, I just showed you how to do that."

"Yeah, but I don't know her number. It was programmed into my old flip phone and couldn't be transferred to my new one," he pouts.

"Well, I'll tell you her number and you can add it to your contacts like I just showed you."

He groans and stares at his phone like he's afraid it will bite him. "What do I have to do again?"

Sigh. "Just give me your phone, Joey."

He hands it to me.

"Are you mad?"

"No." I hold his phone out to him in my outstretched hand.

"Wait, can you add Ric Swift's number for me?" he asks with a sheepish grin.

I look up, surprised. "You're kidding. Really? Are you going to text him? Why?"

"You and your inquisitions," Joey laughs. "Nobody expects the Spanish Inquisition," he says in his best Monty Python voice. "Ric and Natalia are cool. How many cool friends do we have now that Bob and Marcy are in Belize?"

I look at him incredulously. "Joey, Bob and Marcy are not cool. Oh my god. So not cool."

Joey smirks. "They got high and listened to good music," he says. "What other friends do we have who still smoke weed and appreciate the Stones?"

He has a point.

The problem is, that's not the definition of cool anymore, it's the definition of stoner baby boomers. Maybe even laughingstock stoner baby boomers.

But I understand how he feels. I've been a little depressed since Marcy and Bob left to start their new life in Belize. Plus, I've hardly heard from Jazz since Joey returned from Seattle. Christmas is in two weeks and she's said nothing about her holiday plans.

I've had mom vibes for days that she's spending Christmas somewhere on a tropical island with Chaz Chipolata. That's why I haven't just come right out and asked her. I don't want it confirmed. My mom vibes are deadly. I don't know if I've ever been wrong.

Honestly, the only thing that's saved me the past several days is my painting project, working on the Candyland series. I have a whole new appreciation for our home. I've been drowning my sorrows by escaping into the whole creative process for hours every day. I've turned the guest bedroom into a makeshift studio with an easel and all my supplies with dreams of a total remodel and doing it right. The morning light I get in there is spectacular.

Joey continues to work on his pizza skills, which normally would have me excited about visions of Seattle. Instead, I feel dread. He's also been puttering around the garden, and he fixed the shutter that was hanging by a thread. I bet I can talk him into doing a studio remodel for me. Anything that involves art, music, or anything creative, whether it be the garden or the kitchen, he's on board.

It's the drudgery of house repairs I could never interest him in. He honestly doesn't notice chipped plaster, nor does he think it's terrible we haven't painted the house's interior in twenty-five years.

When I was younger, it didn't bother me. I don't know if it's because I'm older, retired, and I'm home all day noticing everything, but I feel cranky that things will never be perfect around here.

Until recently, I had the "We're going to move to Seattle" fantasy, so I didn't let the deteriorating condition of Candyland bother me. Now something has shifted and I'm frustrated all over again.

I feel like we're staying here until we die. There's no place for us in Seattle with Jazz and Chaz Chipolata.

Ugh, Chaz Chipolata. I'm going to have to tell Joey about him. I don't want to, but I can't keep it to myself much longer; it's making me physically and emotionally ill.

I hand Joey back his phone. He immediately starts texting and I have to control myself not to laugh out loud. He's concentrating so hard he's biting his lower lip and struggling with the tiny keyboard. It's hard to believe this is the first time he's tried it, literally almost two decades after everyone else.

I watch him for a few seconds and then have to look away. It's both hilarious and excruciating.

"I just invited Ric and Natalia for dinner next Saturday night. They'll be in Philadelphia for the holidays. You'll love this, they're both vegetarians. Hopefully, Jazz will be here, too. Have you talked to her?"

"No, I haven't," I snap, and even I'm shocked at how nasty I sound.

"What's wrong?" Joey is taken aback. "Are you two having a mother-daughter spat? What did I miss? What happened?"

Now I feel sheepish. "Nothing happened. I guess I've been involved with my painting," I offer through crappy explanation.

"I'll text her," he says, looking at his phone.

"Ha ha, she's going to be shocked. Finally, a text from Dad. She's only been campaigning for this for ten years," I grin.

Meanwhile, I am feeling such trepidation. Joey will ask Jazz about the holidays and what if she tells him the truth?

"Oh, hi, Dad, no, I can't make it for Christmas, I'm going to be in Cancun with my creepy spray-tanned sixty-year-old lover, the guy you call the Pasta King with sarcasm dripping from every pore of your body..."

"I'm going to go upstairs to my studio to work on my painting," I tell him.

Joey raises his eyebrows. "Really? Before I talk to Jazz?" Again, this is not like me.

"Yeah, tell me what she says."

"Stay down here for a few minutes. I might need your help with this thing," he says, still looking at me as if I just told him I'm going to Mars.

Ugh. I sit down on the sofa. Chester jumps up next to me, and I bury my face in his fur and hug him. This conversation will not go well, and at this moment, I want to be anywhere but on the couch.

Joey ends his call and raises his arms in triumph. "Jazz says she's coming home for Christmas," he shouts, though we're only ten feet apart. "She'll be here the morning of the 24th!"

Meanwhile, I'm so unprepared for Jazz's positive response that it doesn't even register for a minute.

"Oh," I reply. I almost said, "Oh, too bad," because I was so sure she wasn't coming. Oh my god. I really have become that person. I can't blame Marcy Garber anymore for this; it's all on me.

"Oh? That's all you have to say? Not only is she coming, but she has a surprise. Someone is coming with her," Joey says with a big smile.

"Who?" Can Joey see I'm about to have a convulsion? Because I'm having one right now. I don't know how my eyeballs are staying in their sockets or how I haven't swallowed my tongue.

"She won't say. But didn't I tell you she's seeing someone? You should have seen her when I was in Seattle. She acted like a teenage girl with a crush," Joey exclaims joyfully.

That's not the sense I got from Jazz about her relationship with Chaz Chipolata. She never seemed giggly or smitten with him. When she described their relationship to me in New York, I believed her. Why would she lie about it being only sexual? That's a big confession to make for no reason. Still, I don't want to call any more attention to myself, so I grab my phone and text Jazz.

> **Dad just told me you'll be here**
> **for Christmas! I'm so excited!**

Jazz texts back immediately.

> **When have I ever not been**
> **home for the holidays?**

Uh…she has a point.

I didn't realize my recent insanity. I noticed it to a point, but I've stopped being present.

I'm doing exactly what I know not to do…one foot in the past and the other in the future.

I text back:

> **You're right. Sorry. So…you are**
> **bringing a guest?**

(Jazz)   **Yep.**

(Me)   **Dad said it's a surprise?**

I wonder if it is the kind of surprise he will have to be restrained from going after with a baseball bat?

(Jazz)   *Yep, it's a surprise.*

(Me)   *I hate surprises.*

(Jazz)   *Mom, don't worry. Everything
              will be fine.*

Jazz adds a bunch of happy face emojis. I resist the urge to reply with a devil emoji.

Or a vomit emoji. Oh my god, she must have gotten engaged to Chaz Chipolata.
Merry fucking Christmas.

"What's she saying?" Joey whines. "Can't I be in on this text, too?"

Woo, thank you Joey. I needed to be snapped back to the present yet again.

"Yeah, you can add in my name when you text Jazz," I respond.

He looks at me like I'm speaking Martian. I grab his phone and show him how. He gives me a big kiss and my heart swells. I love him so much.

Okay, I need to get a grip. This is my favorite time of the year. Enough of this negativity. Joey and I are going to decorate Candyland like Jazz is ten years old and still believes in Santa. I want a ten fucking foot tree. Joey is going to crank out holiday food like he's crazed on steroids and we're gonna wow Ric and Natalia Swift with our hospitality on Saturday night.

Life is good, dammit. I am not Marcy Garber.

Twenty-Four

Natalia and Ric arrive bearing a gaily wrapped gift and two bottles of superb wine.

"Candyland looks so beautiful," Natalia says with shining eyes. "How did I know it would be this magical at Christmas? Didn't I say that to you, Ric?"

"You did," he says, smiling.

Natalia walks over to our tree. "Oh, your ornaments are incredible, too! Everywhere I look, I see something different. I love the twinkling lights in your ceiling! This is why I love this place. What new construction has a sunken two-story living room with a cathedral ceiling?"

"I'm sure if you have enough money, you can build anything," Joey says, looking at them curiously.

"We call new construction 'zombie houses'," Natalia says. "They usually have all white interiors and lots of stainless steel." She shudders. "I could never live anywhere like that. Our home in Nashville is a historic property with all the original features carefully restored."

"Oh, it must be lovely," I say.

"It is," Ric agrees. "It's just too bad it's in a red state."

"Yeah, I don't know how you deal with that," Joey says. He uncorks a bottle of wine and pours us all a glass.

"Merry Christmas, Happy Hanukkah," Joey says, lifting his glass.

We toast and take a sip. This is some seriously excellent wine.

"Nashville is a blue city, though. It's mostly musicians," Ric says. "Have you ever been there?"

"No, I made a vow never to go below the Mason-Dixon line," Joey remarks. "I saw *Easy Rider* when I was thirteen years old and it traumatized me for life."

Ric and I laugh.

What is *Easy Rider*? Natalia asks, looking confused.

"It's a movie from the dark ages, from when Joey and I were kids, starring Peter Fonda and Jack Nicholson as two hippies. They ride across America on motorcycles and see bigotry in our country firsthand when they, um, travel through the south. They end up getting shot to death by two locals in New Orleans," I tell her.

Man, I can't believe she hasn't heard of Easy Rider. Talk about a generation gap.

"I saw it years ago," Ric said. "I used to have the soundtrack on CD when I was a kid. It was probably my grandfather's," he winks.

"Probably," I agree, smiling.

"Yeah, I could see how that movie would color your ideas about the south," Rick continues. "I grew up in California and by the time I got around to seeing *Easy Rider*, I viewed it as a documentary of a tragic time in American history. It didn't have a life-changing effect on me. Well, thanks to Donald Trump and the Pandora's box he opened, the movie is shockingly relevant again, isn't it?"

Joey nods furiously. He loves it when he meets someone who gets him.

I take a sip of wine and smile.

"Natalia, I've been listening to your last record while I work on a painting. I have to tell you, you're inspiring me. Your voice is incredible. Do you have any plans for something new?"

Natalia looks over at Ric and smiles. "Actually, I'm taking next year off from music. We want to start a family."

"That's fantastic! Aw, I'm so happy for you," I gush.

Ric clears his throat. "Yeah, that's when living in a red state will come into play, especially if we have a daughter."

Joey slaps his forehead. "I hear you, brother."

Natalia and Ric exchange a look again. What am I missing here?

Ric sips his wine. "We won't sell our place in Nashville because it's not just an awesome house, it's where I built my studio. But Natalia wants to raise our child at least half the year in Philadelphia, so he or she will benefit from her family," he explains. "Natalia's mom, dad, siblings, and cousins are all here."

"Oh, that's so fabulous," I reply. "Joey, you will have someone else to cook for! I don't say that lightly. Wait until you taste his food. Too cool that you're vegetarians like me. Joey's vegetables are on a whole new level."

Again, Natalia and Ric exchange glances. It's so obvious she is trying to tell him something with

234

her eyes; I'm getting uncomfortable noticing. So naturally I start babbling.

"Joey made pasta with vegetables and feta cheese in a white wine garlic butter sauce for dinner tonight," I say without taking a breath. "For appetizers, he made miniature pizzas…you guys are hungry, I hope."

Ric fans himself like he's pretending to faint, and Natalia says, "Oh, my!"

Joey and I stand there beaming like they're our kids.

"Wait, open our gift first," Natalia insists. "I saw this and thought of you right away!"

No one has to ask me to open a present twice. I rip it open, feeling momentarily guilty about destroying a gorgeous wrapping job.

Their gift takes my breath away. "Oh my god, it's us!" I hold up two ceramic figurines…a woman in jeans and a black shirt, and a man wearing jeans with long hair.

Natalia beams. "They're hippie salt and pepper shakers and as soon as I saw them, I said to Ric, 'Who do these remind you of?' and right away he said 'Joey and Linda!"

"I love them," I say honestly. "Joey, aren't they fabulous?"

He looks at them admiringly. "Indeed," he agrees. "They're great. Let me take them in the kitchen and fill them up so we can use them at dinner. I will return with ze appetizers."

"Do you guys need any help?" Natalia asks.

"Nah, Joey won't even let me help. He's the master of his kitchen," I reply.

"This is true," Joey says. "Be right back."

Joey disappears into the kitchen, and I top off everyone's wine.

"So where in Philadelphia are you guys looking to buy a house?" I ask Ric and Natalia.

"Well, actually…" Natalia begins, but stops and exchanges another look with Ric instead.

"We love this area," Ric says. "This neighborhood, this street. Having Fairmount Park in your backyard is incredible."

"You would live in one of the zombie houses?" I ask, shocked.

Natalia frowns and shakes her head. "Never. "What we are hoping…I mean, what would be perfect for us…is…" her voice trails off and her eyes search out Ric's.

"Natalia is completely enchanted with your house, Linda. She's fallen in love with Candyland," Ric says. "I know we told you we weren't interested in buying the property and that's true, but that's changed since we met you and seen it from the inside. There's a special vibe here. Natalia and I both feel it."

"It would be such an amazing place to raise a child," Natalia says, her voice filled with longing. "A house in the city, yet with acres of Fairmount Park right out the back door. And on a street named for Ric's grandmother." She pauses, a wistful smile on her face. "Jazz told me she had an antique wooden swing set in the yard when she was growing up."

My eyes grow wet at her comment. "Jazz told you that? That's interesting. She made us take it down when she was thirteen so her friends wouldn't think she's a baby. It's still in our garage. We couldn't bear to part with it."

And I talk about Joey's hoarding! I forgot all about the swing. I wonder how much other stuff I couldn't let go of is in the garage.

Natalia claps her hands excitedly. "An antique swing? I would put that back out in the yard tomorrow!" She hugs herself and looks around. "Oh, this house. One thing I promise you, we would never do anything to change it. Any renovations would be merely cosmetic, like installing a granite countertop or some beautiful hand-painted ceramic tiles in the kitchen or…or a magnificent French door to replace the sliding glass patio door…"

I stare at her with my mouth open. I can't even wrap my brain around this.

"We wouldn't even ask, despite how we feel, if Jazz didn't tell us you and she have been scheming to get Joey to sell Candyland and move to Seattle," Ric says, looking apologetic. "Anyway, sorry if we misunderstood or read the situation wrong, but please know if you guys decide to sell, just name your price."

"Five million," Joey announces, walking into the living room with a tray of miniature pizzas.

My head jerks up. How much did he hear? He's smiling. He must have missed the part about Jazz and me scheming.

My palms sweat. I need to change the subject, and I need to do it fast.

Joey puts down his tray on the coffee table. "You are about to have a treat of a lifetime," I wave my hands expansively. "My husband is no ordinary chef."

Ric and Natalia help themselves. It would be a major understatement to say they go nuts over Joey's tiny pizzas.

"These are incredible!" Ric says. "I know you made pasta for dinner tonight, but I could eat a thousand of these. What's the topping?"

"You're eating fontina cheese with roasted red bliss potatoes and rosemary. The other pizza has roasted garlic, grape tomatoes, spinach, and sharp cheddar," Joey says.

I close my eyes to savor the burst of flavor, letting out a contented sigh. "These are the best you have made yet, Joey," I gush. "I love how little and cute they are, but they pack so much flavor."

"Yeah, I can't wait to do these for Jazz's next pop-up event in Seattle," he remarks.

Wait, what? I scratch my head and look at my husband. This is the first of heard of it. "When is Jazz's next pop-up?"

"It's not scheduled yet, but she's hoping to have a bunch of them after the first of the year. We've been hashing out all kinds of ideas," he replied. "While you've been upstairs painting this week, Jazz and I have been texting and planning."

My stomach sinks. Jazz clearly hasn't told Joey about Chaz Chipolata. He wouldn't be planning anything other than Chaz's demise if she had.

Meanwhile, in between practically inhaling Joey's pizza, Ric and Natalia are watching us with obvious interest.

Joey chuckles. "You're just going to stare at me and not ask any more questions?

I give him a look of pure innocence. "Like what?"

"I figured you would try to pump me for information on her surprise, but I swear to you, I have no clue what it is," Joey replies.

Natalia bounces on the couch. "*Ooh,* a surprise! I love surprises."

Normally, I love surprises, too. Just not when they're sixty-year-old weirdos wearing macaroni crowns.

The rest of the evening is a joy. Everyone goes nuts over Joey's pasta. Ric and Natalia almost hyperventilate when Joey produces his famous tiramisu for dessert.

We delve into politics, sharing our mutual disdain for the current president. I try to articulate the experience of being a baby boomer in today's world—a time when the once-hip generation finds itself either ridiculed as a relic of the past or blamed for the world's woes.

"In our minds, we saved the planet by passing laws for equality and initiating practices like recycling. We're as mystified as you are as to what happened to our society," I tell Ric and Natalia. "The hatred between the right and the left is mind-blowing. We're dealing with it by smoking a lot of weed and listening to music, but it's hard," I sigh.

"I would never think of you and Joey as *boomers*," Natalia says without thinking. To her credit, she blushes. "I mean, you seem so much younger."

"We're really nineteen-year-olds trapped in these ancient, decrepit bodies," Joey laughs.

Natalia and Ric, in contrast, are old souls. They're artists. One thing I noticed is that neither one of them looks at their phones whenever they're in our presence.

I have a sudden awful flashback of standing in the dark in Jazz's New York Airbnb and seeing Chaz Chipolata lit up by his phone like a demon.

I gotta text Jazz tomorrow. No way can she spring Chaz on Joey on Christmas Eve.

Twenty-Five

The next morning, I gulp my coffee and head for the studio to work on my latest painting. It will now include a child on an antique swing set as seen out our kitchen window.

Before getting inspired by the Swifts last night, I am not proud to say that I was considering painting another solitary woman in my "Alone in the House" series.

I was going to give her a half-finished, bleeding tattoo.

Yep, I'm in a dark place.

As we went to bed last night, Joey brought up the Swifts' offer to buy Candyland.

"So, what do you think?" he questioned.

"I think we should sell it to them for five million," I replied, burrowing under the blanket and turning on my side away from him.

"Okay, okay, I know you're tired. We'll talk more about this in the morning," he said. "Night. Sleep tight." He kissed the back of my head and shut off the light.

Just a month ago, I would have leaped out of bed to discuss selling Candyland with Joey, even at 2:00 a.m., and practically comatose. Instead, I'm feeling trapped like a rat, wishing I could go hide somewhere.

Joey is going to know something is up. I've been scheming to get him to move to Seattle for over a year. He's going to want to know what changed my mind. But honestly, I have no idea how I'll tell Joey about Chaz. And if I tell him too soon, Christmas could be ruined. But it's not the kind of thing I can leave until the last minute.

I guess I better face it. Christmas this year is screwed no matter what.

But for now, I'm just happy Joey isn't a morning person. He has to be awake for two hours before he has a serious conversation. I manage to slip upstairs and lose myself in my work before the subject of selling Candyland comes up.

I'm just about to take a bathroom break when my phone pings. Oh, too funny. Joey is texting me from downstairs.

We've got some leftover pizza
for lunch. Interested? Miss you.

Oh my god, Joey figured out how to use a heart emoji. How cute is he?

Meanwhile, lunch? I look at the time and am shocked to see it's noon. I've been working for over three hours.

Okay, I guess I can force down some of Joey's pizza.

"Hi," I say, walking into the kitchen. I pinch his butt and he turns and kisses me.

"Hey. How's my artist?"

"Enjoying myself," I reply. "It shocked me when you said it was lunchtime. I lose hours up there when I paint."

Joey opens the oven door and checks on the pizza. "Yeah, I hear you. That's how I get when I'm working in the garden, and now, when I'm working on ideas for the new restaurant. I mean Jazz's new restaurant," he says.

I really can't believe this. My higher power has one hell of a sense of humor.

"Look at you with the new restaurant talk," I say weakly.

"New restaurant in Seattle restaurant talk, even better, huh, Lin?" he replies with a huge smile that freezes and then fades when he sees my reaction.

Have I turned green? I sure feel green, and Joey looks at me like I am.

"What's wrong?" he asks, alarmed. "Are you okay? Are you having an AFib attack?"

"I'm fine. No attack. I…I just got dizzy for a second."

Oh, jeez. I need to watch the drama stuff. The last thing I need is worrying Joey for nothing or being perceived as a hypochondriac…or worse, getting myself set up for a girl who cries wolf scenario.

I keep forgetting I'm sick. Well, not sick, but okay, I have a heart condition. It's the least of my worries, I guess.

You could die.

I hear the words in my head and then firmly extinguish them.

Everyone can die at any moment. That thought should comfort me, but it feels like a ticking clock, amplifying my need to hold everything together—Jazz, Joey, Candyland. The cracks are showing, and I don't know how much longer I can keep them from spreading.

"Linda? You awake? I asked if you want a salad with your pizza," Joey says with a look of concern still on his face.

"Yeah, that would be great," I tell him.

He opens the refrigerator and takes out some lettuce, olives, and tomatoes.

"I have some news," he says, holding the lettuce under running water. "Well, I think it's news, anyway. While you were upstairs, Jazz and I FaceTimed. I love being able to do that, by the way."

"I've only been telling you this for how many years now? That you would love being able to text and FaceTime, I mean. It makes you feel less cut off from society." I can't resist lording it over him.

"Yeah, whatever. I still think people are on their phones too much. You need quiet time…down time…to be creative."

He has a point.

"So what's the news from Jazz?" I ask with total dread.

"It's not news from her, it's about her," he corrects.

"What?"

"Well, I called her at 10:30 our time because I am an idiot who forgot about the time difference. It was only 7:30 a.m. in Seattle," he says.

"Oyyyy, Joey. Why did you call her?"

"I was excited how great the tiny pizzas came out. I think we can either do something with it on the menu or use them at the pop-ups like a wine flight or tasting," he says.

He chops the lettuce on his cutting board and adds it to a big wooden bowl. In goes some avocado, sliced tomatoes, a handful of kalamata olives, and Joey's world-famous mustard vinaigrette. He deftly tosses everything together and distributes it into two salad bowls.

Watching Joey in the kitchen never gets old.

I ignore the "we" when he talks about Jazz's menu. What's that saying about being careful what you wish for?

"Anyway, Jazz was already awake when I called. She was just getting coffee. The big news is, she wasn't alone."

Joey looks at me expectantly, awaiting my excited reaction.

Yeah, good luck with that, Joe. I struggle not to look as queasy as I feel.

"Linda, you're not going to ask me who was with her at her place early in the morning? You're kidding me," he jokes.

"Of course, I want to know! Who was it?" I brace myself, but something's wrong with this picture. Joey's smiling. If he thought Jazz was with Chaz Chipolata, he would freak out; not the good kind of freaking out, more like the King Kong type.

"Well, I'm not one hundred percent sure, but I think it's the guy from the fried chicken restaurant where we had the pop-up," he says. "I only caught a quick glimpse of his face, but he has the same shaggy dark hair, and he's tall and thin. He walked behind Jazz to get coffee. I didn't get a great look, but I saw enough. I told you she was seeing someone. I just didn't know it was the guy from the restaurant."

Wait, what?

"You think you saw Shoki?" I'm trying to process this. Shoki competed with Jazz on *Top American Chef*. I follow him on Instagram. He not only has a wife, he has a brand new baby.

That can't be right.

"I forget his name. Jazz had so many friends who showed up to help," Joey mutters.

"You watched Shoki on *Top American Chef* when he competed with Jazz. So you're saying it's him?"

Joey groans and rolls his eyes. "Do you think I remember who competed in that hot mess?" Joey asks. "I was the one who thought the show was idiotic, and I only watched it to see Jazz. I couldn't tell you who any of the other people are."

I pull up Shoki's Instagram account on my phone and show it to Joey.

"Was it him?"

Joey looks at the pic. "Wait, now I'm not sure. I don't think the guy I saw is Asian. But he had something to do with the restaurant. Why don't you just ask her? What's the big deal?"

I don't know what the big deal is either except I was so sure Jazz's big surprise was Chaz Chipolata I didn't think I had to ask.

Chaz is beefy with reddish hair. He doesn't fit the description.

But wait. What if he lost weight since we last saw him over six months ago, and he just took a shower and his hair was wet so it looked dark? Joey only got a glimpse of a man on a tiny iPhone screen.

Joey's right. I should just ask her.

I'm going to text her right after we get done eating.

Joey brings the salads and pizzas to the table and sets them down. "So after lunch, let's have a family meeting," he suggests.

My head jerks up. Family meetings are serious stuff at Candyland. Joey, Jazz, and I would call for family meetings whenever an issue too big for just one of us to decide arose.

They covered everything from my not being happy about our family vacation plans, to Joey thinking of changing jobs, to Jazz's request (at age thirteen) that Joey and I not smoke weed anymore. A health professional visited her middle school and showed them a short video about lung disease. It wasn't about the weed itself. Luckily, it was right around the time when edibles made the scene.

Family meetings are only called for when the situation is intense and requires deep conversation.

Am I going to try and talk Joey out of moving to Seattle? What's my reason besides some weirdo in a macaroni crown?

"The thing I love about your pizza is, it tastes just as good heated up the next day," I tell him.

"Right? I've really perfected the dough hydration ratio," Joey declares.

"Huh? Explain, please."

Anything to keep the topic off selling Candyland, even if I couldn't care less about dough hydration. I don't even know what it is other than something that has to do with water.

"Dough in the 65-70% hydration range makes for a softer, crispier crust," Joey explains, clearly proud.

"Well, it works," I say, nodding toward the pizza. "It's delicious."

"Thanks," Joey smiles. "I can't wait to make these for Jazz and her friend next week."

Oy. Me, too. Except you're going to want to add hemlock to one of them.

I mean, what are the choices here? A sixty-year-old guy or one with a wife and baby?

More importantly, how much slower can I eat?

Joey runs his hand nervously through his hair, then blurts, "So I'm just gonna come out with it. I think we should sell Candyland to Ric and Natalia."

I almost gag on my pizza. Suddenly it tastes like sawdust. Oh, joy. He's starting the family meeting without announcing it first. If Jazz were here, she'd give him guff for breaking the rules.

Irony never dies at Candyland, huh? Joey looks at me expectantly. But even though I was expecting it, my stomach sinks to my feet and I must look white as a ghost.

Joey frowns and leans closer. "Linda, what's wrong? This is what you wanted. I've been thinking about it nonstop since you had your AFib attack. Then when I went out to Seattle and hung out with Jazz for a few weeks, I knew you were right. The move makes sense on so many levels, even more so now." He sits back and crosses his arms across his chest, clearly expecting an enthusiastic response.

Instead, I stare at him with my mouth hanging open like a dullard.

"What do you mean by 'on so many levels'?" I croak.

"Well, from a practicality level, you and I are getting older. What if something happens to one of us? Do we need the additional stress of being three thousand miles away from our only child? And does Jazz need to be hopping on cross-country flights every time one of us gets sick? But it's more than that…it's like, I was fine the way we've been living since we retired, but it's almost as if…as if we were just sitting around waiting to die."

"Joey! Don't say that!" I'm honestly shocked by his comment. But in a way, I know exactly what he means. We just never said it out loud, other than Joey making a comment like, 'This is the last refrigerator we'll ever buy' or me looking at Chester with a similar thought.

Or Joey not wanting to do even cosmetic repairs to Candyland.

"I mean, I was fine hanging out in our pajamas all day, getting stoned, and watching television reruns of dead people. I thought after over forty years of working full-time, we deserved the rest. And we needed it. But I also can't believe how fast the year went. Our life is just whizzing by now. Before we know it, ten years is going to pass and we'll still be sitting side by side on the sofa, vegging out."

He looks so sad, I want to wrap him in my arms and assure him everything will be okay. And it will be. We just have to take one day at a time.

Joey sighs and continues. "Except one or both of us will probably be sick. Or worse. It's just too sad to contemplate. We don't want to go out that way, do we? Spending whatever time we left watching dead Andy Griffith on *Matlock*?"

He looks at me imploringly. "When I went to Seattle, I can't describe it, I got juiced. It's really beautiful there, and the air is so clean…and working side by side with Jazz, creating menus and just doing our thing…I don't know. I realized I'm not ready to stop living yet. Does that make sense? And I couldn't believe that while I was away, you had the same epiphany and started painting again, but now I'm not sure what you're thinking. My Spidey sense has been telling me something is wrong…"

"Nothing is wrong," I say, or try to say.

"Do you feel okay? You haven't been having heart issues, have you? I'm worried something is bothering you and you're keeping it from me." Joey is upset, and I don't blame him. He's one hundred percent correct. I'm not only acting weird, I'm not telling him how I really feel. If he were doing this to me, I would lose my shit right now.

"I guess all the stuff you said about Candyland got to me," I offer through explanation.

Very weak explanation. If I were on the witness stand, the attorney would lose the case.

Joey frowns and rubs the back of his neck. "You're not even excited about Jazz's new boyfriend. I'm telling you, this looks serious. What if it is? What if there's a grandchild? Don't you want to be part of its life? I don't get why you're not excited. You should see your face. It's like someone died," Joey exclaims. "What's wrong?"

"How do you know Jazz and her new boyfriend won't move to Philadelphia to be near us if they have a baby?" I ask him.

"That's not happening, Linda. Give up the ghost on that one. Jazz loves Seattle. She has a beautiful home there and even though she won't be under contract with Food Television to develop anything new, she'll always be a part of their family and will guest judge and stuff on other food network shows. Not to mention she plans on having total pizza domination there. With us at her side." He stands and begins pacing around the kitchen. "Do you see why I'm so excited now? Jazz wants us to be part of her life."

Oh, my god. Help me, help me, I'm losing my mind. Of course I want what Joey and Jazz want. Probably more than both of them combined. There's just one thing I need to know. Can I take out a hit on Chaz Chipolata?

I sit back and cross my arms against my chest. "I get it, Joey. It's a big step, that's all. I refer back to all your old arguments for never leaving Candyland. The memories where Jazz grew up. Your fear that it will be knocked down and replaced by the LEGO houses, or zombie houses, as Ric and Natalia call them." As soon as the words leave my lips, I realize the error.

"That's just it," Joey explains. "If we sell Candyland to Ric and Natalia, it won't meet that fate. They have the money to lovingly restore it.

And...and we can visit anytime, even if it's just virtual."

I run my hands through my hair, agitated. It's all too much, everything falling into place like this.

With one exception, of course.

I inhale sharply. "Just out of curiosity, Joey, assuming we decide to sell Candyland to the Swifts, what's our asking price? I mean, we joke about five million, but no way in hell we're getting that."

Joey nods. "I've been thinking about that. I think we need to look around Seattle and see the price range for something we like. We don't need anything fancy. I bet we can find something small that's affordable, and Ric and Natalia will work with us. They know we don't want a mortgage at our age."

"I want to talk with Jazz about this," I snap.

Enough of this torture. Jazz must tell Joey about Chaz.

"Okay," Joey consents. "Are we still having the family meeting? Should we FaceTime?"

"You're the one who requested the meeting, not me," I say with a queasy smile. "But let me see if she's free to talk. Don't forget, Candyland is where she grew up. It's her inheritance."

"She doesn't want it. I already ran it by her," Joey says. "But go ahead, talk to her yourself. She'll tell you."

Sigh.

I text Jazz.

> *So did you know Dad wants to move to Seattle?"*

(Jazz) *YES!!!*

(Me)	*Did you also know he wants to sell Candyland to Ric and Natalia Swift?*
(Jazz)	*I KNOW!!! HOW EXCITING IS THAT?*
(Me)	*What's with the all caps? You going all insane Donald Trump on me?*
(Jazz)	*Mom, it's because I'm thrilled beyond belief! This has exceeded all of our wildest dreams. It's almost freakish how everything fell into place. You totally have a higher power. This is sooooo meant to happen.*
(Me)	*Yeah, except you're forgetting one thing, Jazz. How are you going to explain Chaz to your father?*
(Jazz)	*Chaz who?* 😜
(Me)	*The guy your father is going to chase across Seattle with a baseball bat. That Chaz.*

(Jazz)	*Why would Dad do that?*
(Me)	*Jazz...*
(Jazz)	*You are going to make me tell you my surprise, aren't you?*

No, no. No surprises. Not now. I can't deal. But if not now, when?

(Me)	*Okay.*
(Jazz)	*Where is Dad?*
(Me)	*In the kitchen with me.*
(Jazz)	*Okay. I will FaceTime you in just a minute. Are you excited?*

Sweat forms on my upper lip and everywhere else. I haven't had a hot flash like this in over ten years when I went through menopause.

(Me)	*Excited for what?*
(Jazz)	*MY SURPRISE!!!! Get Dad.*
(Me)	*He's here.*

Joey is loading the dishwasher.

"Jazz is going to FaceTime with us in a minute, Joey. She wants to tell us her surprise," I say, rolling my eyes.

"Why are you making that face? It's going to be fine. I'm sure we'll both going to love her new boyfriend," Joey assures me.

"How do you know that's her surprise?" I demand.

"I just know. She kind of told me, and don't ask me what she said. I forget already," Joey admits sheepishly.

"Oh, for fuck's sake, Joey. What good are you?" I am only half-teasing.

My phone rings.

Holy hell, this is it.

I take the call at the kitchen table, prop my phone up against a bottle of ketchup, and put it on speaker. Joey closes the dishwasher door and walks over to stand behind me so he can see the screen, too.

My heart is in my mouth. I can hear it beating in my ears.

"Hi!" Joey and I lean forward into the phone and shout, just like the clueless senior citizens we used to make fun of.

Woo, karma is a bitch when you get old. If you're lucky enough to get old, that is.

Good times, people.

Jazz, meanwhile, thinks it's hilarious.

"Aw, look at you two. You're so adorable. Like little kids," she coos.

Yeah, that's the other thing about getting older. Besides the physical similarities like being bald and toothless as you age, you also get to lose what's left of your mind so you can revert to infancy.

Yay, us.

"Earth to Mom," Jazz says. "Earth to Mom."

Huh? Ugh, I went all Marcy Garber again, didn't I?

"I'm here." I say stiffly.

Joey pretends to slap the top of my head.

"Okay, well, as Dad probably told you, I'm seeing someone. And, um, yeah, it's pretty serious. We're in love. And he's here now, right next to me."

I make this weird, ungodly noise. It's a gulp-snort. Oh my god, did everyone hear, and is a gulp-snort actually a thing? I sounded like a pig rolling around in its trough.

"Mom, are you okay? Now you have to promise to behave and be calm, alright? Don't make a scene. Please don't embarrass me or yourself. Promise?"

"I promise," I reply, a bit impatient.

But why is she making me promise to behave and not Joey?

"And of course we'll both be in Philly for Christmas. I talked with Ric and Natalia, we're going to have one last party at Candyland…anyway, I'm babbling. Ready? Here he is!"

She moves over a bit, and a familiar face fills the screen.

I break my promise that I won't freak out, and I let out a high-pitched scream.

And then I run around the kitchen like a maniac and scream some more.

"I told you this would happen," Jazz remarks.

"What's going on?" Joey asks. "What did I miss here? Why is your mother acting like she did the night you made the *Top American Chef* finale?"

I do a few more crazy woman laps around the kitchen. Thank god, Joey doesn't hold up the phone to show them.

"That's because she knows my fella. You know him, too, you met him at the pop-up in Seattle," Jazz says, laughing. "But okay, I'll introduce you officially, for the second time."

I put my hand over my mouth to keep from squealing anymore.

"Meet my new partner in crime, in life, in everything. He's the absolute love of my life." Jazz puts her arm around him and pulls him closer. "Dad, I'd like you to meet Sean."

Epilogue

Well, I mean, talk about happy endings.

Now if this were really a fairy tale, Jazzy and Natalia would both be giving birth to beautiful bouncing babies right about now and I would be a grandmother and a godmother simultaneously.

All I can tell you is, one is working on it and one is contemplating it.

Pretty cool, huh.

Joey and I are in Seattle, but how crazy is this, we haven't bought a home yet, we're leasing a houseboat. Jazz's awesome friend Sandra, who also lives on Puget Sound, told us about a thirty-foot boat docked on nearby Ballard Canal. Even though Joey and I knew it was nuts, we fell in love with it at first sight. Since we have our eye on new construction that won't be ready for a year, we looked at each other and said "Why the hell not?"

Ric and Natalia were kind enough to take most of our possessions off our hands. They even took the David Bowie action figure. "I love him," Natalia said breathlessly.

So yeah, we're looking at new construction. Us. Can you believe it? But after talking about it extensively, we had to admit that people our age will have an easier time living somewhere that doesn't require any renovation or serious maintenance.

Maybe it's because it's Seattle, but there's a lot of cool new homes here. They're not zombie houses, trust me.

But oh, life on the houseboat is so amazing. When we prop the roof hatch open, we can see the stars from our loft sleeping quarters. It took Chester a few days to get used to it but now he's grooving on the great outdoors. So far we've seen turtles, native and migrating birds, beavers, and otters congregating nearby.

We sure aren't watching Matlock reruns anymore.

Joey is involved neck-deep in Jazz's pizza business. They're planning a brick-and-mortar store early next year. Meanwhile, her catering and delivery service is through the roof successful. They just signed a contract to provide pizza for the Seattle Kraken professional hockey team.

"We'll be able to buy this boat, too, as a vacation home," Joey claims, and he's not joking.

Jazz and Sean are so in love it's magical just being around them. I don't know if I'll ever get over the shock of that phone call and seeing him sitting next to my daughter.

"How? When?" I asked them almost the minute they walked into our house last Christmas Eve.

"Well, we first met at the Food and Wine Festival in New York in April," Jazz said. "We exchanged numbers because even then, we felt something." She smiled at Sean, who literally didn't take his eyes off her.

"And after that, our schedules were so crazy, we couldn't see each other again physically but we texted and talked on the phone for hours. So much of our life intersected, especially our love of cooking from the time we were kids," Jazz said.

"When you told me you were Jazz's mother that day in the restaurant, I couldn't believe it. I ran back into the kitchen and texted Jazz," Sean said. "She didn't believe that you were there, either, so I stealth took your pic and texted it to her."

"I told him not to tell you a word about anything," Jazz laughed. "I warned him about your inquisitions."

He had no idea about my inquisitions, but I spared him the worst of it. I sat there thinking for a moment, adding two and two together.

"So wait. When you were in Philadelphia after I had the AFib attack and you told me you were going out to dinner with friends, was that Sean you were with?" I asked Jazz, wide-eyed.

"Yep," she said, looking at Sean. They both laughed.

"And when you borrowed my black dress that night…"

"Yep!" they both said, looking at each other with such emotion they totally gave away that this was "the" date where they, um, fell in love.

I'm just so damn happy my sexy dress and favorite turquoise bracelet weren't out having a good time with Chaz Chipolata.

After they hooked up in Philadelphia, Sean quit his job, sublet his apartment, and moved to Seattle.

He's another one who fell in love with this city.

In other news, I text Marcy all the time. As Joey predicted, moving to Belize didn't automatically make her happy, and she keeps mentioning her tennis instructor, which makes me very queasy. Yeah, you need to work on changing who you are as a person—where you live, not so much.

Bob is on the golf course 24/7, and Marcy is worried he's involved with sports betting. That wouldn't surprise me. In the pics I saw, Bob looks like he's put on even more weight. For someone out in the sun all day, he's pasty.

Marcy, however, has slimmed down even more and grown her now blonde hair to her shoulders. She's kind of wearing it like I do, which I guess I'll take as a compliment.

Candyland is currently undergoing modest renovations and should be finished in another month or so. Ric and Natalia are planning a big blowout party and you know Joey, Jazz, Sean and I will be there.

Hell, we'll probably do the catering.

On our last day there, Joey and I stood at the threshold for several seconds, struggling to find the words to say goodbye to our home of forty-odd years.

"We're leaving Candyland," Joey finally whispered.

I got so choked up I could barely speak.

And then, for whatever reason, I broke into a cheesy, impromptu version of Hotel California at the top of my lungs with more joyous abandon than I knew I possessed.

Joey joined in. So did Chester.

On the way to the car, Joey put down his suitcase and raced across the front lawn. He grabbed Jazz's Candyland sign by its base and uprooted it from the ground.

"This goes where we go," he said, tucking it under his arm.

Oh, Candyland.

We may have checked out of there, but we can never really leave.

About the Author

Robin Slick is the author of five novels, including a creative fiction memoir, *Daddy Left Me Alone with God.* Her short stories have appeared in *Juked*, *In Posse Review*, *Smokelong Quarterly*, *Opium*, *Word Riot*, *Slow Trains Literary Journal*, and *NFG Magazine*, which nominated Robin' piece "Three Days in New York City" for a Best American Short Story Award. Visit her at **robinslick.com**

Acknowledgements

It had been over ten years since my last published novel, although I had written several in my head, kept a daily blog, and even journaled on Facebook every day during the pandemic and beyond.

And so, I looked to my friends.

I met author Ellen Meister over twenty years ago at Zoetrope.com, an online writers' group founded by Francis Ford Coppola. Ellen has gone on to write ten brilliant, critically acclaimed novels, and not only am I proud to call her my friend, but we have also been beta readers for each other since day one. No one has been more of an inspiration and superhero in my writing life than Ellen, and I encourage everyone to check out her books.

I met Jeri Titus on Twitter the first year of Donald Trump's presidency when the two of us were searching for information and some sort of camaraderie amid all of the divisiveness and chaos in our new world. She would gently ask me about my writing and make me feel guilty for not putting the pen to paper, so I was incredibly proud to shyly email Jeri my very first complete draft of *Leaving Candyland*. I was unprepared for her amazing reaction— all I can say is, it's what motivated me to continue.

My incredible musical family, as always, cheered me on.

And then Debbie Roppolo of Pecan Springs Publishing read the manuscript and not only shared my vision for the book, seemingly shared my brain during the editing process. Between her intelligent, off-beat humor and gentle prodding, we created something special together.

Leaving Candyland is something I am extremely proud of, and I hope you enjoy reading it.

From the bottom of my heart–thank you, thank you, thank you.

www.ingramcontent.com/pod-product-compliance
Lightning Source LLC
Chambersburg PA
CBHW061427040426
42450CB00007B/941